signs and humours

signs and humours

THE POETRY OF MEDICINE

edited by **LAVINIA GREENLAW**

 CALOUSTE GULBENKIAN FOUNDATION

Published by the
Calouste Gulbenkian Foundation
United Kingdom Branch
98 Portland Place
London W1B 1ET
Tel: 020 7908 7604
Email: info@gulbenkian.org.uk
Website: www.gulbenkian.org.uk

Introduction and this selection © 2007 Lavinia Greenlaw
Poems commissioned for this anthology © 2007 Moniza Alvi, Maura Dooley,
Ian Duhig, Grey Gowrie, David Harsent, W.N. Herbert, Kathleen Jamie, Jackie
Kay, Stephen Knight, Michael Laskey, Gwyneth Lewis, Carola Luther, Jamie
McKendrick, Daljit Nagra, Sean O'Brien, Ruth Padel, Richard Price, Denise
Riley, Robin Robertson, Ann Sansom, Jo Shapcott, Greta Stoddart.
For copyright of all other poems see acknowledgements pages 198–202.
The right of Lavinia Greenlaw to be identified as author of the Introduction and
editor of this work has been asserted in accordance with the Copyright, Designs
and Patents Act 1988.

ISBN 978 1 903080 09 2

British Library Cataloguing-in-Publication Data
A catalogue record for this book is available from the British Library

Designed by Helen Swansbourne
Typeset by Helen Robertson
Printed by Expression Printers Ltd, IP23 8HH

Distributed by Central Books, 99 Wallis Road, London E9 5LN
Tel: 0845 458 9911, Fax: 0845 458 9912
Email: orders@centralbooks.com
Website: www.centralbooks.co.uk

Cover: Christine Borland, *From Life (Berlin)*, detail, 1996. Twenty-one glass shelves
with dust traces of human skeleton and spotlights. Installation dimensions
variable. Collection Musée-Château d'Annecy, France. Photo Uwe Walther,
courtesy of the artist and Lisson Gallery, London.

When we throw out waste tissue culture, we may be sure there's always something very small in there calling for help. It's no longer the voice of the tissue culture, the simplified vocal register of life, but rather the whisper of the last, lonely, useless, but nonetheless hopeful hope. No longer really science but still poetry. No longer what is law-carrying, but rather something beyond it, a statistically meaningless and negligible exception.

The incongruous whisper of the last living cell: if you have time, don't discard it; go to the microscope and look at the orphan cellular movement in the dish, and listen.

Miroslav Holub, 'Tissue Culture, or, About the Last Cell', *The Dimension of the Present Moment* (1990), translated by David Young

Contents

Preface

The body is central to preoccupations in the visual arts no less so today than in the past, although the approach now is technological – witness Damien Hirst's obsession with laboratories, forensics, displays of clinical instruments, pharmaceutical taxonomies, animal sections and the skull beneath the skin. The bold sardonic irony may be modern; the poignant sense of *momento mori* is very ancient. More interestingly, however, the work of a number of women artists brings a new kind of questioning to the fore. This may be because women have traditionally been an object in art. Theirs is 'the abject body as a contested site', in the somewhat constricted jargon of psychoanalytical critical theory, more straightforwardly described in John Berger's celebrated book *Ways of Seeing* where he explains how women have learned to objectify themselves, becoming both what he calls the *surveyor* and the *surveyed*, 'The surveyor of woman in herself is male: the surveyed female. Thus she turns herself into an object – and most particularly an object of vision: a sight.'[1]

An engagement with new medical technologies is causing this to change, for men as well as women, for the general public as well as artists. When Helen Chadwick splashed images of her body cells on to epic photographic seascapes, when Mona Hatoum filmed her digestive tract using medical endoscopies and coloscopies for startling walk-in installations, when the French artist Orlan redesigned her face to conform to ideal notions of beauty, allowing herself to be filmed to show the mask of her facial tissues being peeled back to reveal the stuff underneath, there was an exhilarating, if squeamish, sense of self-possession being asserted. Knowledge is power, allowing us to combat fear, as if we can collude with the physicians to see ourselves as fascinating physical specimens rather than helpless sufferers. Doctors may sigh when patients arrive in the surgery full of new knowledge about their condition acquired from the internet, but this is surely better than continuing to feel an inchoate synthesis of terror and bewilderment. It may even be therapeutic.

Many of the poems in this new anthology play with the boundaries between the self as subject and object, as observed and observer, using language, as only poets can, to convey both the immediacy of pain and sensation, and a driven intellectual curiosity about cause and effect. Lavinia Greenlaw is the ideal editor for such a collection. A sensitive and accomplished poet herself (she is also a novelist and art historian), she has long been drawn to science and particularly to medical imagery and vocabulary. She comes from a family of doctors and was exposed to countless medical discussions from early childhood. In 2005 she undertook a residency at the Royal Society of Medicine, which provides continuing medical education and accredited courses for all kinds of healthcare professionals, where she commissioned some of Britain's leading contemporary poets, somewhat bizarrely asking them to choose the medical condition that most interested them, and then found specialist clinicians or medical researchers to inform their understanding. Out of these, 22 new poems are published here for the first time. As Lavinia Greenlaw comments in her introduction, all are drawn to investigate the felt sense of the unwell body, but all, too, bring an objective medical understanding to the task. To complete the anthology she has selected existing poems from the past and present which explore similar themes.

This is not a book for the faint-hearted. If it is read sequentially, it might well be regarded as compendium of fear. But anthologies are meant to be dipped into and many many individual poems address the profound sensation of being alive, not ill; curious, not defeated; good-humoured, not pathetic. It is an impressive, energising and vigorous collection.

SIÂN EDE
Arts Director, Calouste Gulbenkian Foundation

1. John Berger, *Ways of Seeing*, p. 47 (London, BBC and Penguin Books, 1972).

Introduction

'How are you?' This question, which we ask of each other all the time is often more of a gesture than a true enquiry, and is met as such. It is, like so much of the codified talk around illness, a kind of dance step or semaphore. In John Berryman's 'Dream Song 207', which opens this anthology, this reflexive enquiry is addressed head-on – 'How am I?' – and in that moment, a psychological trapdoor opens.

> – How are you? – Fine, fine. (I have tears unshed,
> There is here near the bottom of my chest
> a loop of cold, on the right.
> A thing hurts somewhere up left in my head.
> I have a gang of old sins unconfessed.
> I shovel out of sight
>
> a many-ills else ...)

The answer describes a self doubly in parenthesis: 'I am not going to tell you how I feel,' and 'I do not feel myself.' When we experience this kind of dislocation, we can feel that we no longer inhabit ourselves or that what we inhabit is no longer our self. Language attends to this: as C.K. Williams notes, we *fall* ill, a passive act suggesting a loss of ground. It is as if when unwell, we fall through the floor of ourselves.

The arrest and interruption caused by illness are part of a broader experience of arrest and interruption, of 'something going wrong with the equipment of the world'[1] which forces us to reconsider the familiar. Illness is an acute version of this: something going wrong with the equipment of the self. As Valerio Magrelli says: 'Things that work are muffled/and mute – their parts just move.' What goes wrong might be something as small as in this case a facial tic, but we notice it and we stop and reconsider the whole self – ours or someone else's. This imperative born out of interruption is also in the impulse towards poetry: the moment in which preconception is denied us and we must experience something dis-equipped.

Signs and Humours is not arranged chronologically. I have endeavoured to show how the same experience and questions, the same confounding sensations, have been part of the poet's engagement with the physical self for thousands of years. Medicine is a science, but it also belongs to a general field of human enquiry which encompasses poetry. Both begin in the self and neither escapes it. So here is Thomas Hardy admiring the persistence of genes, and, two thousand years apart, Lucretius and Richard Price contemplating sleep.

The medical issues and conditions of our age reflect its concerns and pressures. There are poems here about Alzheimer's, autism, Post-Traumatic Stress Disorder, insomnia, anorexia, depression and sleep medicine, fertility treatment, neuroscience, and HIV/AIDS. Sarah Maguire's poem about Chernobyl, 'May Day, 1986', has lost none of its potency in twenty years. The air is still 'uncertain'.

The book takes its title, *Signs and Humours*, from Denise Riley's poem 'Pancreas, Liver, Biliary Tract' in which she observes the ways doctors still read signs – urine, blood, complexion, bile – and how we, the patients, strain to read the doctors. So much of medicine is about the interpretation of the image, be it x-ray, mammogram, MRI or ultrasound. And we find it hard to stop ourselves reading into such images, as when Susan Wicks sees the blood vessels of her eye as 'deer and bison running/in their red cave.'

Chaucer praises the physician's 'natural magic' ('magyk natureel') which resides not only in diagnosis but in the cure, often in the form of medicine. Remedies encompass everything from pills to herbs to a dose of radiation; it might take the form of talking and touch. We invest medicine with meaning just as we invest signs and images. Ian Duhig's 'The Plague Journal' suggests that when we have no cure, we might invent one, and it might work:

Later our food became medicine: dried fig-grubs for the
    incontinence;
ant-lions in sake for the headaches;
leek-leaves and cucumber for the burns.

We live within 'the narrow bed of our flesh' (Zbigniew Herbert),
no more so than when, say, in a high fever or entering depression or
negotiating a broken bone. The acutely unwell person withdraws into
themselves. The world is their body, their pain. Robert Burns is as
outraged by mockery of his toothache as by the toothache itself.
Horace wonders what he has done to deserve terrible indigestion
brought on by garlic while Robert Lowell's response to eye trouble is
characteristically epic. Jonathan Swift laments falling sick after having
just moved to Ireland and so having none of his loved ones there to
make a fuss.

It seems that the more conscious we become of how we operate in
the world, the more aware we are of our physical presence. The
mathematician and philosopher Alfred North Whitehead noted the
'"withness" of the body', a phrase which situates our physical selves
in relation to our consciousness rather than as part of it:

Sense-perception of the contemporary world is accompanied by
perception of the 'withness' of the body. It is this withness that
makes the body the starting point of our knowledge of the
circumambient world.[2]

We still, in many ways, measure the world according to ourselves
but our relation to our bodies has become estranged even as we
investigate, medicate and operate upon it. It is as if the more we see
of it, the further back we have to stand in order to take in the view.
James Lasdun fixes on Nabokov's 'delicate meeting place between
imagination and knowledge'[3] to describe the experience of being
confronted by a vial of his own blood. One might say that the body
is just such a place: as we inhabit our bodies, we are forced to imagine
them. Williams issues another warning:

> Be cautious of your body, which isn't you,
> though neither are you its precise other;
> you're what it feels ...

This is a tricky relation and one which can easily go wrong, throwing our whole selves out of joint. Berryman describes how 'the whole matter breaks down/or would it would...' a sense of extrapolating dysfunction which means that when we go wrong, our relation to the world goes wrong too.

This situation calls for a mode of articulation which will accommodate rupture, an expressive structure which puts in place the experience of being out of place. Poetry is suited to this. It offers a coherence of sensation rather than of meaning and its structures are more a form of pure arrangement than an organism or a machine. A poem is achieved through equilibrium, as is health. Our bodies are a balancing act as John Armstrong says: 'so mutable the state of man.'

Perhaps because we now have the technology to see through our bodies, deep into the earth and far out into space, we forget that, 'All kinds of things in outsides are enclos'd' (Lucretius). Yet when our own boundaries are ruptured, we become more aware of them rather than less. We are reminded that we are more likely to go wrong than not. In his *Anatomy of Melancholy*, Robert Burton cites Catullus: 'Man that is born of a woman, is of short continuance, and full of trouble.'[4] We forget how 'full of trouble' we are until our containments are breached.

The loss of sleep is a fundamental loss of boundary as in Charles Simic's 'Hotel Insomnia' with its fractured thinking, its confusion of interior and exterior:

> Once, too, the sound of a child sobbing.
> So near it was, I thought
> For a moment, I was sobbing myself.

The most absolute border is that between life and death and this book could have been filled by poems on that subject alone. What I have looked for were those which consider what it means to cross the border into being, and being *here*, as described in Paul Muldoon's

'Birth' with its inventory of wonders, and the way in which life knits itself out of association and resonance from the first in Andrew Motion's 'Natural Causes', or the separation described in Victoria Redel's 'Ninth Month':

> Already the world, the world.
> And you are slipping
> down, away from my heart.

Emily Dickinson famously said that a poem should take the top of your head off. She also said: 'when I try to organize – my little Force explodes'. Dickinson had a particularly fine sense of the relationship in poetry between explosiveness and organisation, and how this could accommodate the extremities of experience where other forms of articulation break down. This is most forcefully in evidence here in poems written by those in the knowledge of their own coming death: Raymond Carver and Julia Darling.

If there were a phrasebook for illness, it would feature such expressions as 'I am not quite myself,' and 'feeling out of sorts'. In illness we are not ourselves and yet trapped in ourselves. As James Wright puts it: 'I have lain alien in myself so long.' Poetry activates all that is liminal and residual in language, and so perhaps can best express this condition. It can be simply put, as in William Cowper's nineteenth-century account of paranoia which ends with the image of being 'Buried above ground' – dead and alive at the same time. Others, too, describe the experience of psychiatric disorder as if being horribly suspended between states. Wallace Stevens's 'Depression in Spring' cuts off action from reaction in a profound disconnect:

> The cock crows
> But no queen rises.

The world contracts, in the case of William Carlos Williams's poem, to a 'recognizable image', a picture on his sick-room wall. D.H. Lawrence complains of the 'sick grapes', dust and cobwebs which surround him. While they are describing stasis, others use contraction as a response to chronic and terminal diagnoses. Julia

Darling's 'Chemotherapy' employs its submission to the sonnet form to reflect that 'I never thought that life could get this small', the regulation iambic pentameter of the line bringing to mind a ticking clock but also a caged animal rocking or a trapped thought. Simon Armitage uses the sonnet to similar inexorable effect to observe the effects of ankylosing spondilitis, in which 'my skeleton will set like biscuit overnight.' The sestina is another strict form, six verses with recurring end-words, and Caitríona O'Reilly uses it in 'Thin' to confront the trap of an eating disorder. Repetition and the slipping use of 'bone', 'glass', 'skin' etc., reduce these objects to their essential meaning and sensory effects. Gerard Woodward chooses the villanelle, so tight a form it usually throttles itself, to describe hypnotism in a mesmerising vortex.

The confinement of illness can bring a sharp appreciation of the world, prompting the depth of focus and disturbance of perception which are instrumental in poetry. Dorothy Wordsworth valiantly insists she can get as much pleasure from her memories as from striding the hills, while Emily Dickinson speaks of how:

> One earns by measuring the Grave –
> Then – measuring the Sun –

There is a further breakage in illness – that between others and ourselves. It is most obvious in the awkwardness and sensitivity which enters language. People don't know what to say and so revert to basics. 'How are you?' 'It hurts.' Miroslav Holub, the Czech poet and immunologist, begins a poem with Wittgenstein's observation that the statement 'It hurts' has replaced our moans and groans. As Holub says, this word 'pain' is 'a pretence of silence'. It's not saying nothing, but it is saying something in a way that withholds itself.

When contemplating another's mortality, we can experience a tense combination of empathy and self-preservation. The tradition of the elegy acknowledges this in its convention that the poet, while lauding the dead, is asserting a right to life. Philip Larkin describes how glimpsing a patient being stretchered into an ambulance makes us 'sense the solving emptiness/That lies just under all we do'. It is our own death we contemplate, unable to escape ourselves even when in tremendous grief for the loss of someone else.

Illness can disarm us entirely, as in Raymond Carver's 'What The Doctor Said' in which he is being told that he will die of lung cancer. Absorbing this information reduces him to platitudes:

> I jumped up and shook hands with this man who'd just given me
> something no one else on earth had given me
> I may even have thanked him habit being so strong

The broken-down nature of this experience is reflected in a poem which is unpunctuated and unstoppable, with all the moods passed through in this brief exchange steamrollered into a single inexorable fact. At the same time each line is self-contained; each a step in the process of absorbing this knowledge and attempting to make sense of it.

Illness can engender poetry (from the writhing Horace to the Victorian invalid Elizabeth Barrett Browning to the manic Robert Lowell) and it may be that a significant proportion of poets experience psychiatric disorders, but good poetry will be written in spite of illness, not because of it. In the ninth century, the Chinese poet Po Chü-I, lying bored and unwell in bed, can't stop himself writing poetry, even though he knows it will be 'slight and flavourless'.

Shakespeare is one of many who have used the body as metaphor, here to analyse the nature of power in an extract from *Coriolanus* in which Menenius defends the importance of the belly:

> The strongest nerves and small inferior veins
> From me receive that natural competency
> Whereby they live.

In 'Sonnet 147', Shakespeare complicates the conventional image of love's fevers. We use the imagery of illness, and we invest illness with significance and association yet, as Susan Sontag says, 'illness is *not* a metaphor.'[5]

The body and the map have long been analogous. Countries are drawn to look like people and the body is described as a country, here by Phineas Fletcher who distinguishes the function and nature of veins, arteries and nerves through the metaphor of fountains and rivers. Miroslav Holub looks through the microscope at 'dreaming landscapes,/lunar, derelict' only of course they are not derelict at all but seething with implication: the murmuring 'revolt of immense estates'.

The imagery of medicine can be dangerously colourful. Robin Robertson's 'Seagull Murmur' is a proper medical term and the exact description of a cardiac malfunction. How else to describe something strange other than in terms of the familiar? Anthonis van Leeuwenhoek, the radical sixteenth-century scientist, was the first person to see globules of blood under the microscope lens and could only describe them as being like grains of sand on black taffeta.

Of course, poetry responds to the language of medicine and the force of its imagery, and not just the traditional or the historical. New disciplines such as neuropsychology and the study of autism bring new concepts and so new language. Traditional imagery persists but here, where a poet does compare something to a flower, it is the smell of phenic acid in the anatomy room, which reminds Gesualdo Manzella-Frontini of autumn amaryllises. Beautiful yes, but that suggestion of acridity and rot is also beautifully exact.

Poetry is discourse too and several of the works included here are an attempt to assert or make sense of something. Mary Carey writes in 1657 of her miscarriage, agonisingly trying to make sense of what has happened within the rigorous framework of her faith. Ruth Padel enters the physiology of the mosquito in order to explain not what malaria is but why it exists. This more roundabout investigation gives more insight into a cure than the straightforward consideration of symptoms.

Some poets might seem to be making a virtue out of illness but most pursue the experience to interrogate rather than to celebrate it. Even when Marin Sorescu says: 'I don't feel ill in order to feel better,/I feel ill in order to feel worse,' he is not indulging in bravado but questioning the true nature of this experience and his response to it. Sylvia Plath, always far more in control than her reputation might suggest, describes the grandeur of high fever: 'I am too pure for you or anyone.' She is not enjoying this but giving an accurate depiction of an unbearably acute super-human state in which she is all light and heat, 'flickering, off, on, off, on'.

Collapse, crisis, danger and loss have the effect of wiping away detail and making us stop and think. Pliny is optimistic that 'In sickness the mind reflects upon itself, with judgment surveys itself, and abhors its former courses.'[6] Until it recovers, that is. Recovery is a relatively undramatic state and so there are far fewer poems about getting better than there are about falling ill. Robert Lowell returns home after treatment for mania to a frail continuity of domestic routine. He knows that he has lost a kind of magnficence: 'Cured, I am frizzled, stale and small.' The joy of recovery, our own or that of others, may not last but it marks a return from Berryman's parenthesis, from the broken down, turned-up world of the unwell:

> there is this great kindness everywhere:
> now in the grace of the world and always. (*Tom Paulin*)

It is a moment that passes more quickly than we realise and so seems like the right place for this book to come to a stop.

LAVINIA GREENLAW

1. Heidegger's phrase as used by Mark Kingwell in 'Husserl's Sense of Wonder', *The Philosophical Forum*, vol. XXXI, no. 1, Spring 2000.
2. Alfred North Whitehead, *Process and Reality* (1929).
3. Vladimir Nabokov, *Speak, Memory* (1967).
4. Robert Burton, *The Anatomy of Melancholy* (1621).
5. Susan Sontag, *Illness as Metaphor and AIDS and Its Metaphors* (1979).
6. *In morbo recolligit se animus*, Pliny, cited in Robert Burton, *The Anatomy of Melancholy* (1621).

signs and humours

JOHN BERRYMAN

Dream Song 207

– How are you? – Fine, fine. (I have tears unshed,
There is here near the bottom of my chest
a loop of cold, on the right.
A thing hurts somewhere up left in my head.
I have a gang of old sins unconfessed.
I shovel out of sight

a many-ills else, I might mention too,
such as her leaving and my hopeless book.
No more of that, my friend.
It's good of you to ask and) How are you?
(Music comes painful as a happy look
to a system nearing an end

or an empty question slides to a standstill
while the drums increase inside an empty skull
and the whole matter breaks down
or would it would, had Henry left his will
but that went sideways sprawling, collapsed & dull.)
How are you, I say with a frown.

FRED D'AGUIAR

Airy Hall Ward

There will be days when you or I are bedridden,
Unable to stomach direct light or a voice.
Who fly-posts town?
Word spreads faster than the virus
Rusting the joints; weeks' worth of picked fruit
Turns the whole place into an orchard.

It's enough to make anyone get up.
All this loving and understanding
That's just there for when
You're in a bad way
And all the time I'm thinking
They must have the wrong address altogether:

The door-knocker that had to be silenced
With a bandage, the children shooed
From the sick part of the house –
Partitioned, horticulturally sound,
And a solid stillness
You had to whisper in and labour through.

MIROSLAV HOLUB

Brief reflection on the word Pain

Wittgenstein says: the words 'It hurts' have replaced
   tears and cries of pain. The word 'Pain'
   does not describe the expression of pain but replaces it.
   Thus it creates a new behaviour pattern
   in the case of pain.

The word enters between us and the pain
   like a pretence of silence.
   It is a silencing. It is a needle
   unpicking the stitch
   between blood and clay.

The word is the first small step
   to freedom
   from oneself.

In case others
   are present.

translated by Ewald Osers

PO CHÜ-I

from Illness and Idleness

Illness and idleness give me much leisure.
What do I do with my leisure, when it comes?
I cannot bring myself to discard inkstone and brush;
Now and then I make a new poem.
When the poem is made, it is slight and flavourless,
A thing of derision to almost every one.
Superior people will be pained at the flatness of the metre.
Common people will hate the plainness of the words.
I sing it to myself, then stop and think about it ...

translated by Arthur Waley

VALERIO MAGRELLI

The Tic

Gestures that go astray
appeal to me – the one
who trips up or upturns
a glass of ... the one who forgets,
is miles away, the sentry
with the insubordinate eyelid
– my heart goes out
to all of them, all who betray
the unmistakeable
whirr and clunk
of the bust contraption.
Things that work are muffled
and mute – their parts just move.
Here instead the gadgetry,
the mesh of cogs, has given up
the ghost – a bit sticks out,
breaks off, declares itself.
Inside something throbs.

translated by Jamie McKendrick

SIMON ARMITAGE

Splinter

Was it a fall in pressure or some upward force
that went to the head of that spikelet of glass
and drew it through flesh, caused it to show its face
so many years to the day after the great crash.

THOMAS HARDY

Heredity

I am the family face;
Flesh perishes, I live on,
Projecting trait and trace
Through time to times anon,
And leaping from place to place
Over oblivion.

The years-heired feature that can
In curve and voice and eye
Despise the human span
Of durance – that is I;
The eternal thing in man,
That heeds no call to die.

ROGER McGOUGH

Oxygen

I am the very air
you breathe
Your first
and last
breath

I welcomed you
at birth
Shall bid
farewell
at death

I am the Kiss of Life
Its ebb and flow
With your last gasp
You will call my name:
'o o o o o o o o'

ROBERT BURNS

Address to the Tooth-Ache

My curse on your envenom'd stang,
That shoots my tortur'd gums alang,
An thro' my lugs gies mony a bang
      Wi' gnawing vengeance;
Tearing my nerves wi' bitter twang,
      Like racking engines.

A' down my beard the slavers trickle,
I cast the wee stools owre the meikle,
While round the fire the hav'rels keckle,
      To see me loup;
I curse an' ban, an' wish a heckle
      Were i' their doup.

Whan fevers burn, or agues freeze us,
Rheumatics gnaw, or colics squeeze us,
Our neebors sympathize, to ease us,
      Wi' pitying moan;
But thou – the hell o' a' diseases,
      They mock our groan.

O' a' the numerous human dools,
Ill har'sts, daft bargains, *cutty-stools*,
Or worthy friends laid i' the mools,
      Sad sight to see!
The tricks o' knaves, or fash o' fools,
      Thou bear'st the gree.

Whare'er that place be, priests ca' hell,
Whare a' the tones o' mis'ry yell,
An' plagues in ranked numbers tell
        In deadly raw,
Thou, *Tooth-ache*, surely bear'st the bell
        Aboon them a'!

O! thou grim mischief-makin chiel,
That gars the notes o' discord squeel,
Till human-kind aft dance a reel
        In gore a shoe thick,
Gie a' the faes o' Scotland's weal
        A TOWMOND'S TOOTH-ACHE!

hav'rel, *halfwit*; heckle, *flax-comb*; cutty-stool, *stool of repentance in church*;
mools, *grave-clods*; gree, *supremacy*; towmond, *twelvemonth*

LEONTIA FLYNN

Acts of Faith

On my 24th birthday
my lungs close over, tight as a baby's fist
round its first rattle.
It might be the Holy Ghost,
the disc of light skittering on the ceiling
thrown up from the paten on a water-glass
which my mother brings with Prednisone.
She sings Happy Birthday Happy Birthday
and tells me, as she has always done,
that she would take my place. I believe her.

ROBERT HASS

A Story about the Body

The young composer, working that summer at an artists' colony,
had watched her for a week. She was Japanese, a painter, almost
sixty, and he thought he was in love with her. He loved her work,
and her work was like the way she moved her body, used her
hands, looked at him directly when she made amused and
considered answers to his questions. One night, walking back
from a concert, they came to her door and she turned to him
and said, 'I think you would like to have me. I would like that
too, but I must tell you that I have had a double mastectomy,'
and when he didn't understand, 'I've lost both my breasts.'
The radiance that he had carried around in his belly and chest
cavity – like music – withered very quickly, and he made himself
look at her when he said, 'I'm sorry. I don't think I could.'
He walked back to his own cabin through the pines, and in the
morning he found a small blue bowl on the porch outside his
door. It looked to be full of rose petals, but he found when he
picked it up that the rose petals were on top; the rest of the bowl
– she must have swept them from the corners of her studio –
was full of dead bees.

HORACE

Epodes 3

He whose impious hand has strangled
his aged father deserves to eat it. It is
more harmful than hemlock. Garlic.
Peasants must have iron guts.
What venom rages in my gizzard?
Have these roots been stewed
in vipers' blood without my knowledge?
Has Canidia handled this evil dish?
Medea infatuate with the Argonauts' captain
(more fair than all his crew)
when he tried to yoke the unbroken bulls
anointed her Jason with this;
and before she fled on the great winged worm
she took revenge on his mistress
by making her gifts besmeared with this.
Never did such a fiery, stifling heat
settle on drought-parched Apulia.
Nessus' shirt did not sear
more swelteringly into
resourceful Hercules' shoulders.
If ever you are tempted this way again,
my humorous Maecenas, I devoutly hope
that your girl will push away your face
and retreat to the very edge of the bed.

translated by W.G. Shepherd

JACKIE KAY

My Face is a Map

I was born with a map of Australia on my face;
It was beautiful, my mother told me,
There was nobody like me in the whole wide world,
Who could trace the edges of down under
On the raised and grafted song lines of her face.

I was connected to the upside down people,
To the people who loved the bush and the kangaroo.
I could never smile or frown or weep
In case my special map fell off my face.
My face was pulled so tight so that nobody got lost.

I held my head steady and I held my head high.
When people gaped and gawped and gawked
I thought they were trying to find Alice Springs,
To work out where they wanted to go, where they'd been.
And when somebody stared for a very long time

I would simply ask if they had been down under:
the hardest human heart melts when it sees a koala bear.
My words were slower than other children's
Because my map was stitched to my mouth:
every time I managed a whole sentence,

I imagined a small boat floating out of Sydney harbour.
Yesterday, there was talk of taking my map off,
changing my face so that it looks like others;
My mother said I should have a long think,
And that maybe life would be easier ...

I am thinking now, staring hard into the mirror.
I trace the hard edges of the world in my face.
I know the hard stares of some people.
Without my map, will I be the same person?
Will I know where I am, where I have been?

SELIMA HILL

from The Inpatient, Chapter 3: Doctors

The patients rise like early morning milk.
The planets' movements alternate the tides.
The waiting-room. It frightens me. The hole.
DISEASES OF THE MIND. Pet monkeys. Silk.

Wild bees know little joy.
No visitors.
I've wanted to go home all my life.
Moving deeper into purple woodland.
Lop-eared rabbits, walnuts. Wearing boots.
Ginger weasels cross the gated road.
The little dog is limping.
So am I.
My mother says I'm hopeless.
Bits of lettuce.
The doctor wrote it down:
'Her haunted mind.'

JAMES LASDUN

Plague Years

*There is, it would seem, in the dimensional scale of the world, a kind
of delicate meeting place between imagination and knowledge, a point,
arrived at by diminishing larger things and enlarging small ones, that
is intrinsically artistic.*

VLADIMIR NABOKOV, Speak, Memory

Sore throat, persistent cough ... The campus doctor
Tells me 'just to be safe' to take the test.
The clinic protocol seems to insist
On an ironic calm. I hold my fear.
He draws a vial of blood for the City Lab,
I have to take it there, but first I teach
A class on Nabokov. Midway I reach
Into my bag for *Speak, Memory*, and grab
The hot bright vial instead. I seem at once
Wrenched from the quizzical faces of my class
Into some silent ante-room of hell:
The 'delicate meeting place'; I feel it pounce;
Terror – my life impacted in the glass
My death enormous in its scarlet grail.

ROBERT PINSKY

from Essay on Psychiatrists

IV. A Lakeside Identification

Yes, crazy to suppose one could describe them –
And yet, there was this incident: at the local beach
Clouds of professors and the husbands of professors

Swam, dabbled or stood to talk with arms folded
Gazing at the lake ... and one of the few townsfolk there,
With no faculty status – a matter-of-fact, competent,

Catholic woman of twenty-seven with five children
And a first-rate body – pointed her finger
At the back of one certain man and asked me,

'Is that guy a psychiatrist?' and by god he was! 'Yes,'
She said, 'He *looks* like a psychiatrist.'
Grown quiet, I looked at his pink back, and thought.

V. Physical Comparison with Professors and Others

Pink and a bit soft-bodied, with a somewhat jazzy
Middle-class bathing suit and sandy sideburns, to me
He looked from the back like one more professor.

And from the front, too – the boyish, unformed carriage
Which foreigners always note in American men, combined
As in a professor with that liberal, quizzical,

Articulate gaze so unlike the more focused, more
Tolerant expression worn by a man of action (surgeon,
Salesman, athlete). On closer inspection was there,

Perhaps, a self-satisfied or benign air, a studied
Gentleness toward the child whose hand he held loosely?
Absurd to speculate; but then – the woman saw *something*.

The Pathologist

Pinkish brown, frilled
like a sea-thing, the body-part
your surgeon excised
lies on my cutting block.

It's strange you can't sense
my trained gaze, or the pressure
as my fingers squeeze
the slubby lymph-nodes

of your colon, or my scalpel
pare from a breast-lump
samples to be fixed,
stained pink, beautified.

My task is to scrutinise
that which is rendered unto me –
see: through a microscope
how a smear of tissue

drawn from your small intestine
contains great kingdoms:
like an airman, I look down
on promontories, fiords,

miles of hinterland.
Thus, tender inquisitor,
I detect the dumb
conspiracies of cancer,

pin-point the root
causes of pain: the trials
you'll soon endure
I help prescribe.

We shan't meet – I diagnose
but do not bear
difficult news, preferring
to work quietly, at one remove.

RAYMOND CARVER

What the Doctor Said

He said it doesn't look good
he said it looks bad in fact real bad
he said I counted thirty-two of them on one lung before
I quit counting them
I said I'm glad I wouldn't want to know
about any more being there than that
he said are you a religious man do you kneel down
in forest groves and let yourself ask for help
when you come to a waterfall
mist blowing against your face and arms
do you stop and ask for understanding at those moments
I said not yet but I intend to start today
he said I'm real sorry he said
I wish I had some other kind of news to give you
I said Amen and he said something else
I didn't catch and not knowing what else to do
and not wanting him to have to repeat it
and me to have to fully digest it
I just looked at him
for a minute and he looked back and it was then
I jumped up and shook hands with this man who'd just given me
something no one else on earth had ever given me
I may even have thanked him habit being so strong

MARY CAREY

Upon the sight of my abortive birth the 31st December 1657

What birth is this, a poor despisèd creature?
   A little embryo, void of life, and feature.

Seven times I went my time, when mercy giving
   deliverance unto me and mine, all living.

Strong, right proportioned, lovely girls and boys,
   their father's, mother's present, hoped-for joys.

That was great wisdom, goodness, power, love, praise
   to my dear Lord, lovely in all his ways.

This is no less. The same God hath it done.
   Submits my heart: that's better than a son.

In giving, taking, stroking, striking, still
   His glory and my good is His my will

In that then, this now, both, good God most mild,
   His will's more dear to me than any child.

I also joy, that God hath gained one more
   To praise him in the heavens than was before,

And that this babe, as well as all the rest,
   since it had a soul, shall be for ever blest.

That I'm made instrumental to both these –
    God's praise, babe's bliss – it highly doth me please.

Maybe the Lord looks for more thankfulness
    and high esteem for those I do possess.

As limners draw dead shades for to set forth
    their lively colours and their pictures' worth,

So doth my God, in this as all things wise,
    By my dead formless babe teach me to prize

My living pretty pair, Nat and Bethia,
    the children dear God yet lends to Maria.

Praise be His name. This two's full compensation
    For all that's gone and that in expectation,

And if herein God hath fulfilled his will,
    His hand-maid's pleased, completely happy still.

I only now desire of my sweet God
    the reason why He took in hand His rod.

What He doth spy? what is the thing amiss?
    I fain would learn whilst I the rod do kiss.

Methinks I hear God's voice, 'This is thy sin,'
    (And conscience justifies the same within)

'Thou often dost present me with dead fruit.
    Why should not my returns, thy presents suit?

'Dead duties, prayers, praises, thou dost bring,
    affections dead, dead heart in everything,

'In hearing, reading, conference, meditation,
  in acting, graces and in conversation.

'Who's taught or bettered by you? No relation.
  Thou art cause of mourning, not of imitation.

'Thou dost not answer what great means I give.
  My word, and ordinances do teach to live.

'Lively, oh do it.' Thy mercies are most sweet,
  Chastisements sharp and all the means that's meet.

'Mend now my child, and lively fruit bring me,
  so thou advantaged much by this wilt be.'

My dearest Lord, Thy charge and more is true.
  I see it, am humbled, and for pardon sue.

In Christ forgive and henceforth I will be –
  'What?' Nothing, Lord: but what Thou makest me.

I am nought, have nought, can do nothing but sin,
  as my experience saith, for I've been in

Several conditions, trials great and many.
  In all I find my nothingness; not any-

Thing do I own but sin. Christ is my all,
  that I do want, can crave; or ever shall.

That good that suiteth all my whole desires
  and for me unto God, all he requires,

It is in Christ. He's mine, and I am His.
  This union is my only happiness;

But, Lord, since I'm a child by mercy free,
  Let me by filial fruits much honour Thee.

I'm the branch of the vine. Purge me therefore,
  Father, more fruit to bring than heretofore.

A plant in God's house, Oh! that I may be,
  more flourishing in age, a growing tree.

Let not my heart, as doth my womb, miscarry,
  but, precious means received, let it tarry

Till it be formed of gospel's shape and suit,
  my means, my mercies, and be pleasant fruit.

In my whole life, lively do thou make me.
  For Thy praise and name's sake, Oh, quicken me!

Lord, I beg quickening grace. That grace afford!
  Quicken me, Lord, according to Thy Word.

It is a lovely boon I make to Thee.
  After Thy loving kindness, quicken me.

Thy quickening spirit unto me convey;
  and thereby quicken me, in Thine own way.

And let the presence of Thy spirit dear
  be witnessed by His fruits. Let them appear

To, for Thee; love, joy, peace, gentleness,
  long-suffering, goodness, faith and much meekness.

And let my walking in the Spirit say,
  I live in it and desire it to obey,

And since my heart Thou'st lifted up to Thee,
   amend it Lord, and keep it still with Thee.

saith Maria Carey
always in Christ happy.

January 12th, 1658

DAVID HARSENT

Tinnitus

to Alan Palacci

All night on the beach. A crush
of pebbles. The clop and splash
of waves on a groyne. Mish-mash
of jetsam. Just the place
for my father's barnacled face
to wash up. The clash and hiss
of water makes me miss
most of what he says:
something like 'tosh' or 'fash' or 'fish'.

* * *

In another country a man
falls from a tall building
or a rock, perhaps, with a rep
for just that sort of thing.

His cry is carried to you,
unravelled, by a wind
that travelled step by step
or else hand over hand
mile after mile after mile

for days on end.

* * *

What if the music of the spheres
were the cryptic *ne plus ultra* of human fears ...

* * *

I am walking down a lane that is white with dust.
It could be a dream; it could be the dream will last,
unlike any shape or shade of love you care
to name (or find and follow if you must).

Empty, white with dust, and something stopless in the air:
the chain-stitch of cicadas; a dynamo somewhere.

* * *

Largo, allegro, con brio, glissando, crescendo,
vivace, veloce, da capo, da capo, da capo.

* * *

A single note drawn out
beyond imagining,
pitched for a dog or a rat
by a man with a single string
on a busted violin.

Easy to see that his penance
for gall is never to let
the music settle to silence.

* * *

Something indelible behind your eyes:
the swift's wide wall-of-death between
the campanile of San Giovanni Battista
and balconies filled with flowers, a seamless scream
flowing behind the bird, a tiny twister
too sharp and shrill to be anything but lies.

* * *

Rough music in the lane,
the love-child lapped in blood
and safe at her breast, the pain
echoed in wood on wood,
steel on steel, as they come,
the women in their blacks,
to hound her from house and home,
bands of bitches and claques
of crones with their pots and pans,
their hooks and ladles and bowls,
to beat outside in the street,
to stand at her window and howl,
while the child takes a taste of green
milk and 'the dead of night'
is all she has of her own
and the music goes on and on.

ROBIN ROBERTSON

A Seagull Murmur

is what they called it,
shaking their heads
like trawlermen;

the mewling sound of a leaking heart
the sound
of a gull trapped in his chest.

To let it out
they ran a cut down his belly
like a fish, his open ribs

the ribs of a boat;
and they closed him,
wired him shut.

Caulked and sea-worthy now
with his new valve; its metal
tapping away:

the dull clink
of a signal-buoy
or a beak at the bars of a cage.

JAMES WRIGHT

A Prayer in My Sickness

La muerta entra y sale

You hear the long roll of the plunging ground,
The whistle of stones, the quail's cry in the grass.
I stammer like a bird, I rasp like stone,
I mutter, with gray hands upon my face.
The earth blurs, beyond me, into dark.
Spinning in such bewildered sleep, I need
To know you, whirring above me, when I wake.
Come down. Come down. I lie afraid.
I have lain alien in my self so long,
How can I understand love's angry tongue?

DOROTHY WORDSWORTH

Thoughts on My Sick-Bed

And has the remnant of my life
Been pilfered of this sunny spring?
And have its own prelusive sounds
Touched in my heart no echoing string?

Ah! say not so! The hidden life
Couchant within this feeble frame
Hath been enriched by kindred gifts.
That, undesired, unsought-for, came.

With joyful heart in youthful days,
When each fresh season in its round
I welcomed the earliest celandine
Glittering upon the mossy ground.

With busy eyes I pierced the lane,
In quest of known and unknown things,
The primrose a lamp on its fortress rock,
The silent butterfly spreading its wings,

The violet betrayed by its noiseless breath,
The daffodil dancing in the breeze,
The carolling thrush, on his naked perch,
Towering above the naked trees.

Our cottage-hearth no longer our home,
Companions of nature were we,
The stirring, the still, the loquacious, the mute –
To all we gave our sympathy.

Yet never in those careless days
When spring-time in rock, field, or bower
Was but a fountain of earthly hope,
A promise of fruits and the splendid flower,

No! then I never felt a bliss
That might with that compare
Which piercing to my couch of rest,
Came on the vernal air.

When loving friends an offering brought,
The first flowers of the year,
Culled from the precincts of our home,
From nooks to memory dear.

With some sad thoughts the work was done,
Unprompted and unbidden,
But joy it brought to my hidden life,
To consciousness no longer hidden.

I felt a power unfelt before,
Controlling weakness, languor, pain.
It bore me to the terrace walk –
I trod the hills again.

No prisoner in this lonely room,
I saw the green banks of the Wye,
Recalling thy prophetic words,
Bard, brother, friend from infancy!

No need of motion, or of strength,
Or even the breathing air:
I thought of Nature's loveliest scenes,
And with memory I was there.

JAMIE McKENDRICK

Darkness Tangible

In medias res of the magnum opus
– when *dink!* lights out, the screen went down:
I pressed the line bar, Ctrl/Alt/Esc,
checked the plug, the wires, the works, but zilch.
The room itself had darkened with the dusk
I hadn't noticed falling. I hit the lightswitch
but the dark stayed on. Same with the lamp. *Power cut,*
it dawned on me. The road outside
which might as well have been a wood
had gone mute with tactile dark, a feral,
airless depth of dark. As I patted the floor
for a matchbox or a plastic lighter
my heart was beating faster than it ought to
and the beat had changed as though the peaks
of alps had been rubbed away by time
to docile fluttering undulations – mere hills
at best – and the big firm clockwork current
that ran across its glistening chambers was diverted
into a host of small errant paths that petered out.

I saw my heart as a hut of lap larch
with a torn roof of mastic'd felt
almost flat-packed with the sudden pressure...
Though there was the lighter. My calloused thumb
spun the treadwheel but the spark had gone –
its midget flint expired in peppery dust.
Then I came across a matchbox
but stuffed to its roof with squiggly fagends
and the odd, laid-out, char-headed match,
rough to the touch like a dwarf asteroid.

At last my hands alighted on a candle
I must have put there for emergencies
though of what use now when even the lighter
had, it feebly struck me, now become a darker.
I saw its no flame lifting from the copper aperture
like a huge cypress, and with the black candle
still in my hand I started walking down the stairs
to the cellar where in the furthest corner
I still believed the glowing fusebox hung.

Alzheimer's

Chairs move by themselves, and books.
Grandchildren visit, stand
new and nameless, their faces' puzzles
missing pieces. She's like a fish

in deep ocean, its body made of light.
She floats through rooms, through
my eyes, an old woman bereft
of chronicle, the parable of her life.

And though she's almost a child
there's still blood between us:
I passed through her to arrive.
So I protect her from knives,

stairs, from the street that calls
as rivers do, a summons to walk away,
to follow. And dress her,
demonstrate how buttons work,

when she sometimes looks up
and says my name, the sound arriving
like the trill of a bird so rare
it's rumored no longer to exist.

IAN HAMILTON

The Visit

They've let me walk with you
As far as this high wall. The placid smiles
Of our new friends, the old incurables,
Pursue us lovingly.
Their boyish, suntanned heads,
Their ancient arms
Outstretched, belong to you.

Although your head still burns
Your hands remember me.

JULIA DARLING

Chemotherapy

I did not imagine being bald
at forty-four. I didn't have a plan.
Perhaps a scar or two from growing old,
hot flushes. I'd sit fluttering a fan.

But I am bald, and hardly ever walk
by day, I'm the invalid of these rooms,
stirring soups, awake in the half dark,
not answering the phone when it rings.

I never thought that life could get this small,
that I would care so much about a cup,
the taste of tea, the texture of a shawl,
and whether or not I should get up.

I'm not unhappy. I have learnt to drift
and sip. The smallest things are gifts.

to my last period

well girl, goodbye,
after thirty-eight years.
thirty-eight years and you
never arrived
splendid in your red dress
without trouble for me
somewhere, somehow.

now it is done,
and I feel just like
the grandmothers who,
after the hussy has gone,
sit holding her photograph
and sighing, *wasn't she*
beautiful? wasn't she beautiful?

D.H. LAWRENCE

Malade

The sick grapes on the chair by the bed lie prone; at the window
The tassel of the blind swings constantly, tapping the pane
As the air moves in.

The room is the hollow rind of a fruit, a gourd
Scooped out and bare, where a spider,
Folded in its legs as in a bed,
Lies on the dust, watching where there is nothing to see
        but dusky walls.

And if the day outside were mine! What is the day
But a grey cave, with great grey spider-cloths hanging
Low from the roof, and the wet dust falling softly from them
Over the wet dark rocks, the houses, and over
The spiders with white faces, that scuttle on the floor of the cave!

Ah, but I am ill, and it is still raining, coldly raining!

RUTH PADEL

The Origins of Malaria

1

'OK little one,' God said to the anopheline mosquito.
'The word is glucose.' God looked round. Marvels
were still to come. He was getting there but the devil
was in the detail, deadline near. 'What I've reserved
for you's unnoticed sweetness. Bounty in small doses

where others never go. This place is *garden*. Horizontals
in these leaves hold dew, rain, snowmelt, sweat
of chlorophyl. Follow them. Be cyclical.
Lay eggs' (a beat of silence as silver-stripe female
quivered in blue air) 'in dabble of standing water.

Be good at finding it. I give you the gift
of piercing surface very gently. At first the kids
will be aquatic. Larvae, pupae sort of thing. Suddenly
they'll hatch, grow wings: a cycle of becoming
I worked out specially for you. And in everything I give'

(God looked fondly at high-wire bentfeather legs
more delicate than any created being was likely to invent
or invent well – *look* at those touch-pads and spiracles!
He'd taken trouble, hadn't He, in His miniaturist
phase?) 'is the gift of not being noticed.

Never mind the browngold giants underneath
these trees. What I'm giving you looks small
but there's one design feature I think you'll like:
a mechanism to adjust: go on and on adapting all
the other gifts I've given. So, here. All yours.'

2

But something happened. Put it how you will:
we all carve out our own place in the temple.
One afternoon came a river of new wind.
Drowsing between two glucose blueprints

on a fig-tree, *anopheles* saw light change
for ever. No more world as it was promised. Glad
of their sticky feet, they clung to the underside
of leaf. Tree tried to fling them off.

They'd never worried about snakes. Mustard coils
of sleeping cobras were only good for resting on.
Closed skin of hardening apples, same. Nor
were swords a problem. God had given them

thirst for plant juice: sap, not symbols.
And angels passed them by: *garden* buzzed all day
with angel paparazzi. But they were made,
they found, to be afraid of flame.

3

When two-legs went from *garden* they left too.
Chemistry, along with gravity, had changed.
On a suddenly impure planet, female now craved

two-legs' presence. Something else, she felt,
was needed to lay eggs that'd really *live*: red
cells, plasma with a tang only these warmbloods

possessed. Subterfuge appeared. The male
watched, surprised, and stuck to glucose.
Nothing had changed for him but where she was.

Taking her due was easy despite the donors' first
invention: covering skin. There was a side effect
but tiny, like every other mosquito thing. She never drank

from the same spot twice, took only what she must.
She discovered a gift for camouflage: under-tray
of the pickle-seller, wrinkle in the sheet, plaited vine

on the mud hut's wall, glob of varnish on the lute.
Small, as God had sort-of said, meant hidden.
Though He had also given, or someone had, a whine.

4

In shining ochre grass, downstream of God's
abandoned workshop, rose a ribboned leafsnake.
(God had gone to town on herpetology; each one,
from skeletal armature to interstitial scales,
a miracle of craft.) He hectored the unused atoms,

jealous sparks from God's cooling anvil. All of us
have something we've forgotten to clear up.
His bifurcated tongue flicked out at gut
of *anopheles* female: so little and – yes –
beautifully wrought. 'Now's your chance!

D'you want to stay inert discardings from the out-tray
all your lives? Model yourselves on that mosquito.
Create a cycle inside hers which His not-noticing
design will never see. You won't harm *her*. Make free
of her purloined haemoglobin! Assemble in

her salivary gland and replicate through fission.
Be genus *plasmodium*, one-celled sporozoa.
Look – I can penetrate brains: the power
two-legs has for naming comes from me. So
I pronounce you *protozoa*! Firstlife! Parasite.'

In Sickness

Written soon after the Author's coming to live in Ireland, *upon the Queen's Death,* October 1714

'Tis true – then why should I repine,
To see my Life so fast decline?
But, why obscurely here alone?
Where I am neither lov'd nor known.
My State of Health none care to learn;
My Life is here no Soul's Concern.
And, those with whom I now converse,
Without a Tear will tend my Herse.
Remov'd from kind *Arbuthnot*'s Aid,
Who knows his Art but not the Trade;
Preferring his Regard for me
Before his Credit or his Fee.
Some formal Visits, Looks, and Words,
What meer Humanity affords,
I meet perhaps from three or four,
From whom I once expected more;
Which those who tend the sick for pay
Can act as decently as they.
But, no obliging, tender Friend
To help at my approaching End,
My Life is now a burthen grown
To others, e'er it be my own.

Ye formal Weepers for the Sick,
In your last Offices be quick:
And spare my absent Friends the Grief
To hear, yet give me no Relief;
Expir'd To-day, entomb'd To-morrow,
When known, will save a double Sorrow.

WALLACE STEVENS

Depression Before Spring

The cock crows
But no queen rises.

The hair of my blonde
Is dazzling,
As the spittle of cows
Threading the wind.

Ho! Ho!

But ki-ki-ri-ki
Brings no rou-cou,
No rou-cou-cou.

But no queen comes
In slipper green.

VICTORIA REDEL

Ninth Month

Already you are moving down.

Already your floating head
engaged in the inlet
from where you will head out.

Already the world, the world.

And you are slipping
down, away from my heart.

Sonnet 147

My love is as a fever longing still
For that which longer nurseth the disease,
Feeding on that which doth preserve the ill,
Th' uncertain sickly appetite to please:
My reason the physician to my love,
Angry that his prescriptions are not kept
Hath left me, and I desperate now approve,
Desire is death, which physic did except.
Past cure I am, now reason is past care,
And frantic-mad with evermore unrest,
My thoughts and my discourse as mad men's are,
At random from the truth vainly expressed.
   For I have sworn thee fair, and thought thee bright,
   Who art as black as hell, as dark as night.

DENISE RILEY

Pancreas, Liver, Biliary Tract

i] The patient who had no insides

As clouds swell to damply fill gaps in mountains, so in
Illness we sense, solidly, our entrails expanding to stuff
That space of our innerness just feebly imagined before.

I'd slumped at home before the nightly documentaries
Of scalpels nipping through the primrose fat, beaded
With that orange hue that blood becomes, on camera

But only when they crossly assert themselves do those
Guts I hadn't believed in, truly come home in me.
Have *you* got insides, do you feel? Figuratively, yes

We've guts; literally, may suspect we haven't, poking
Gingerly like Doubting Thomases, feeling our gaps
Not our thicknesses. Thick innerness in us we doubt –

Until ... Madness to dream we haven't any depths
Yet what's packed below skin we don't see laid bare.
Invaginated folds, ballooning orifices, we know about

And pregnancy, watching some unborn other's heels
Nudging and butting like carp snouts under the navel.
That's someone else altogether, palpable inside me.

No, it's my disbelief in my own entrails that I mean.
I'd glimpsed the radiographer's dark film, starring
Barium-whitened swags of colon, mine. Blown glass,

Hooped entrails ridged with their glazed diverticules
Like little suckers studded plumply on squid tentacles
Of my intestines. But now I see their outer evidence:

My ginger skin. How well you look, they'd said to me
At work. But no tan browned my face; it was the malady
Conveyed an air of robust health through bronzing me.

ii] On the ward of signs and humours

Now foamy bracken-brown urine cools in plastic jugs
For measuring on the ward, frothed like a hillside stream
Relaxing into pools. 'What says the doctor to my water?'[i]

Jaundice is read as if the humours still remained reliable.
There *were* insides inside me – now they've gone all wrong.
Modern regimes of signs set in and newly prudent thoughts

That what they stamp, we own. Pointers to a depth, to be
'Philosophically, Medicinally, Historically open'd & cut up.'[ii]
From Burton's ripe account of melancholy, that last quote.

The sorrows brood inside our purplish spleens, barriers
That check dark moods of sultry bile by segregating it
Where it can't seep to hurt us. Anatomized emotion.

'Pancreas' means 'all flesh'. Now, awry, it chews itself.
That piece of ambient meat I am eats meaty me all up.
Enzymes flood to champ their host, their prey – that's

Me. They don't know where to stop.[iii] I'm auto-gesting,
Spontaneous combustion in a schlock Victorian engraving
Of hearthrug scorched, charred ankles jutting out of boots,

For notes see page 186.

No more of faithful Lizzie left. A hapless autophage I am
Whose fizziog's gone bad. Enzymes digesting tissue grind
In rampant amylase and swollen lipase counts. Sure signs[iv]

Affecting the liver, a plush nursery for the vegetal spirit.
Fondly this warming organ clasps the stomach set over it
Fingering heat into it, nursing its charge, so Galen held.[v]

Flame-like, this liver, slow-cooking the stomach's stuff
Down to a bloodlike juice. Not boiling it dry to char it,
Or simmering it into gruel, if the liver's temper is right.

Noble the strong liver, 'dark monarch' to Neruda[vi]
But ignoble, the long slim pear of the gallbladder
And the sole-like spleen, roughened, its shoe shape

Splayed into an ox tongue.[vii] Spleen, milky-pulped
Innocent home to the darkest of humours, frees all
Merriment in its bearer, by holding black bile apart

And so, wrote Harvey, 'the spleen causes one to laugh'.
Dreaming of red things, the sanguine man keeps bluff,
Night shades held safely at bay.[viii] Splenetic laughter!

Liquid the humoured body awash in blood and phlegm
Its yellow and black bile straining for proper harmony
In a weekend supplement conceit of 'healthy balance'.[ix]

Still surreptitiously active, humoural medicine turned
On gauging those measures which plotted our temper;
Better choleric fiery bile than the dryly saturnine black.

'Remembering mine affliction and my misery,
The wormwood and the gall.'[x] So cries *Lamentations*
Too harsh on the house of that yellow emulsifier,[xi]

Hard, too, on wormwood, a friend boiled to absinthe
To smoky Verlaine, and the maker of Pernod's fortune.
Antique are that shrubby vermifuge's properties: bitter

Carminative, anthelmintic, cholagogue, febrifuge,
Swelling the secretions of both liver and gall bladder.
Bluish or red-brown skin markings today? Bad signs.[xii]

iii] To theatre

A table waits beneath a Kubrick set of purple TV screens.
It's for my ERCP, standing (as I won't ever learn) for
Endoscopic retrograde cholangiopancreaticography.

'You'll be so zonked in surgery you won't recall a thing'
Breezed the surgeon, matronly in his j-cloth theatre cap.
Triumphantly I find I do, and heard them as they work:

'Acute pancreatitis, emergency admission, female, 57'
Relayed into a dictaphone, unglamorous summary.
Strapped tightly into place, head cool from its sedation

I wonder who they mean – Oh yes. Brisk chat of
Twickenham while they gouge, debride, and do swift
Housework in my biliary duct, vacuuming biliary sludge.

Like spirit scrambled from her grave on Judgment Day
Poised in Recovery, upright on my trolley, I survey
The tight blue chrysalids of others. Blanketed sleepers.

iv] The patient longs to know

Back on the ward, the darting housemen, veering,
Swerve low by ends of beds like swifts, but then zoom off.
Come back! the impatient patient wails, though silently,

Why am I 'nil by mouth' for endless days? Am I each day
Prepped for some other op which never comes – or what?
Unreadable as a leaving lover, no houseman stops to say.

'Your notes got lost so we might send you back, pre-op.
Without your write-up, no, the anaesthetist won't like it.'
My starved heart sinks at hearing this; it's bodily starved

Like all the rest of me, so long on 'nil by mouth'. Nil
In my own mouth, yes, to eat or drink – but also nil
Issued as word of explanation from a doctor's mouth.

Let me get home so I can find things out. Googling
Fulfils the nineteenth century's dream of ardent enquiry
Amassed, and nearly democratically. On medics' sites

The grand Miltonic phrases of the biliary tract race home:
Islets of Langerhans, Ampulla of Vatter, Duct of Santorini,
Sphincter of Oddi. Sonorous names, some the narrowings

Which, blocked, will cause grave trouble. They had for me
Whose gall bladder, choked, must go. But will its ghost
Kick up in me, once it is tossed away? This oddness of

Owning spare parts. Our bodies littered with redundancies
Walking reliquaries rattling our appendices, blunt tails,
Primordial. For we are birds with teeth and empty crops.

v] The consultant summarises our national health

'Liver, until so recently the Cinderella of medicine!
Just the girl in the clinical ashes, unrescued as yet
Assailed by her bad suitors – weak policies and folly.

'Alcohol-led liver failure rising, bile duct cancer rates
Mounting, more cirrhosis from viral illness, Hep B, C.
More drinking, younger drinking, increased steatosis,

'Yet funders don't cough up for self-induced sickness.
Specialists get scarcer, beds vanish, bureaucracy swells
As need begs for new transplants, more artificial livers.

'One gets despondent. Lifestyle's the problem', adds
This eminent hepatologist, 'despondent at patching up
Self-harming patients, worsened by government policy.'

His time is short. This patient nods and leaves. Maybe
It is a national fantasy, not just my private idiocy
That what our daily intake is by mouth has nil effect.[xiii]

vi] In the next bed

One night the crash team thunders down the ward like a herd of buffalo,
shouting eagerly, piling in dozens and dozens of them, wild, breathless, to
the cubicle of the elderly lady in the next bed who thinks, her daughter has said,
the hospital are trying to kill her. She's from Kabul, had been huddled and
swathed under her bedclothes, glaring, fearful, like an injured eagle. The
crash team works fiercely, reinforcements whoop and clatter in. Machinery
pounds and clanks. Out they tumble before dawn through the thin chintz
curtains, laughing, race on to the next near-death. Mad gaiety of self-protection.
Early morning, her second collapse, the running team crowd back in. In at
the kill. Rattle of the crash trolleys again. Medical students, crammed in to
be quizzed around her, answer: I wouldn't resuscitate her again, too poor a
prognosis – are told, Wrong, we can't not RST her, it's because we can't find
the consultant to sign her off, it's pointless clinically but we have to go ahead,
for Chrissake someone tidy up this mess before anyone lets her relatives in,
someone keep them in the day room. Then they storm out, leaving the last
hours of her stertorous breathing, and a sobbing daughter. Her son-in-law,
embarrassed, standing aside: We all have to go some day, it's as Allah wants,
but my wife loves her mother, she's upset, you see.

vii] Discharged

'Your liver tests are squiffy, Mrs R, but you might
As well go home, you won't get well in here' – then
He's darted off again, mercurial houseman. Outside

The well ones all charge past us like young bullocks
Amazingly confident. Those who were ill go gingerly.
A smack of post-ward colour shoves them back to life

From solitude cells, to watch what's fat with presence.
One plain small thing, a lumbering bee, can captivate
Or fig shoots by a wall. Unannexed lives re-start.

PO CHÜ-I

Illness

Written c. AD 842, when he was paralysed

Dear friends, there is no cause for so much sympathy.
I shall certainly manage from time to time to take my walks abroad.
All that matters is an active mind, what is the use of feet?
By land one can ride in a carrying chair; by water be rowed in a boat.

translated by Arthur Waley

BENJAMIN PÉRET

Little Song of the Disabled

Lend me your arm
to replace my leg
The rats ate it for me
at Verdun
at Verdun
I ate a lot of rats
but they didn't give me back my leg
and that's why I was given the CROIX DE GUERRE
and a wooden leg
and a wooden leg

translated by David Gascoyne

CAROLA LUTHER

'I watch the bees slow down the summer'

I watch the bees slow down the summer. Honeysuckle sink
beneath their substance. Yellow busbies stuffed with sleep
and ochre powder making journeys, wavery, vague,
full of just-remembered purpose, so I come to think
of geriatric gardeners, with their pots and hats and secret
pockets full of dust, casting stuff on yellow air so seconds
stretch (a whole, long, summer each, if we could only enter them)
a gift of sorts, for us, a hunch, as if they've guessed, the bees,
and understood the rock at the garden's end, the crouching
sky, the path on its narrow belly, dropping to the sea.

SHARON OLDS

His Stillness

The doctor said to my father, 'You asked me
to tell you when nothing more could be done.
That's what I'm telling you now.' My father
sat quite still, as he always did,
especially not moving his eyes. I had thought
he would rave if he understood he would die,
wave his arms and cry out. He sat up,
thin, and clean, in his clean gown,
like a holy man. The doctor said,
'There are things we can do which might give you time,
but we cannot cure you.' My father said,
'Thank you.' And he sat, motionless, alone,
with the dignity of a foreign leader.
I sat beside him. This was my father.
He had known he was mortal. I had feared they would have to
tie him down. I had not remembered
he had always held still and kept quiet to bear things,
the liquor a way to keep still. I had not
known him. My father had dignity. At the
end of his life his life began
to wake in me.

ROBERT LOWELL

Waking in the Blue

The night attendant, a B.U. sophomore,
rouses from the mare's-nest of his drowsy head
propped on *The Meaning of Meaning*.
He catwalks down our corridor.
Azure day
makes my agonized blue window bleaker.
Crows maunder on the petrified freeway.
Absence! My heart grows tense
as though a harpoon were sparring for the kill.
('This is the house for the mentally ill.')

What use is my sense of humour?
I grin at 'Stanley', now sunk in his sixties,
once a Harvard all-American fullback,
(if such were possible!)
still hoarding the build of a boy in his twenties,
as he soaks, a ramrod
with the muscle of a seal
in his long tub,
vaguely urinous from the Victorian plumbing.
A kingly granite profile in a crimson golf-cap,
worn all day, all night,
he thinks only of his figure,
of slimming on sherbert and ginger ale –
more cut off from words than a seal.

This is the way day breaks in Bowditch Hall at McLean's;
the hooded night lights bring out 'Bobbie',
Porcellian '29,
a replica of Louis XVI
without the wig –
redolent and roly-poly as a sperm whale,
as he swashbuckles about in his birthday suit
and horses at chairs.

These victorious figures of bravado ossified young.

In between the limits of day,
hours and hours go by under the crew haircuts
and slightly too little nonsensical bachelor twinkle
of the Roman Catholic attendants.
(There are no Mayflower
screwballs in the Catholic Church.)

After a hearty New England breakfast,
I weigh two hundred pounds
this morning. Cock of the walk,
I strut in my turtle-necked French sailor's jersey
before the metal shaving mirrors,
and see the shaky future grow familiar
in the pinched, indigenous faces
of these thoroughbred mental cases,
twice my age and half my weight.
We are all old-timers,
each of us holds a locked razor.

LUCY HUTCHINSON

from Translation of *De rerum natura* ('On the Nature of the Universe') by Lucretius

This excerpt is from Book IV, describing the causes of and necessity for sleep

All kind of things in outsides are enclos'd
Either a callous skin, or bark, or shell,
Through which air pierces, and the same as well
Assails the inward parts, to whose dark seats
With the respired breath it entrance gets.
Therefore th'air ent'ring bodies, both these ways,
While it the strokes through our small pores conveys
To our first seeds, which life's springs there assail,
The members by degrees begin to fail,
And the positions of the seeds which do
Body and mind compose, are shaken so,
That part of the soul's vigour is expird,
Part of it to the inmost holds retir'd,
Part, in the limbs disperst, cannot rejoyne
The rest, nor there in mutual acts combine.
Thus nature's ways being stopped, they cannot meet,
Since with changed motions makes a close retreat;
Then the deserted body feeble lies,
Each member languisheth, the heavy eyes
Hang downe their lids, the flagging arms no strength
Retain, the limber thighs lie stretched at length.
Againe sleepe follows eating, for what th'air
Works on the body, meats do also there,
Flowing through the veins, the like effects beget;
And those sleeps are the most profound which meat
Or wearinesse infuse, because then many seeds
Confounded, greater perturbation breeds,

And inwarder retreat of soul effects,
More of the spirits through the pores ejects,
More scatters those which in the body stay,
And makes them at a wilder distance stray.

MIROSLAV HOLUB

In the Microscope

Here too are dreaming landscapes,
lunar, derelict.
Here too are the masses,
tillers of the soil.
And cells, fighters
who lay down their lives
for a song.

Here too are cemeteries,
fame and snow.
And I hear murmuring,
the revolt of immense estates.

translated by Ian Milner

GREY GOWRIE

Local

Shrub scrub
between Radiography
and where nurses live;

our small sub-
wood: stage flat with two or three
beech, one silvery

birch, holly and laurel and then
the fox mangy lawn
beyond Outpatients – we thrive

on natural scraps:
slivers, like these;
like the halogen

mist of a moon
over Pharmacy;
the drowsy syrups

Tramadol, Zopiclone
which blind night ache,
or the borrowed sun

in our north-faced room
fooling the mind's eye and heart's care
that summer when

the E Ward woodpecker
did strut and take
light on his breast and burst into green fire.

IAN DUHIG

love me little

on the school ranch holidays
hands called me/ *slo mo, echolally & veg*
when it rained & we/ had to play cards & i repeated what they said,
went out of order & twisted when i was bust. but
they got nice in time,
talking with me in the sun
as   i   bounced   round   the   paddock   on   ponies.
teachers,
on the other hand/ were always telling me to REFRAIN
from saying this/ &/ that that
i shouldn't have.
(hands don't
hiss/ REFRAIN so much as shout/ DUMBSONOFA
when i let stuff out/ i shouldn't have
like secrets or horses).

dumb, i got to love words &
where they rode in from. *refrain*
's from the latin for/ *bridle* (not my path
i've found) & means:
a recurring phrase in a poem or/ song. i found when
phrases recur in poems or songs nobody got angry,
so i got to love them too. *burden* is another word for *refrain*:
love me little, love me long:
that's the burden of my song
a ranch hand sang (he called me his burden). a hand's song. a poet's
singing hand: leaves in keats'.

teachers told me my/ mind was all
over the place, that i/ had no
CENTRAL COHERENCE.
now i'd reply/ that if i twig leaf
not trunk it means my thinking is
not 'arborescent' but
'r   h   i   z   o   m   a   t   i   c'
& in poetry i surely know/ my pot80s &
if i'm slow/ my vegetable love
shall grow/ vaster than empires.

i showed you my hand(s):
give me your hand.

SIMON ARMITAGE

from Book of Matches

æŋkɪˈləʊzɪŋ spɒndɪˈlaɪtɪs:
ankylosing meaning bond or join,
and spondilitis meaning of the bone or spine.
That half explains the cracks and clicks,
the clockwork of my joints and discs,
the ratchet of my hips. I'm fossilizing –
every time I rest
I let the gristle knit, weave, mesh.

My dear, my skeleton will set like biscuit overnight,
like glass, like ice, and you can choose
to snap me back to life before first light,
or let me laze until
the shape I take becomes the shape I keep.

Don't leave me be. Don't let me sleep.

JOHN BETJEMAN

Devonshire Street, W.1.

The heavy mahogany door with its wrought-iron screen
   Shuts. And the sound is rich, sympathetic, discreet.
The sun still shines on this eighteenth-century scene
   With Edwardian faience adornment — Devonshire Street.

No hope. And the X-ray photographs under his arm
   Confirm the message. His wife stands timidly by.
The opposite brick-built house looks lofty and calm
   Its chimneys steady against the mackerel sky.

No hope. And the iron knob of this palisade
   So cold to the touch, is luckier now than he
'Oh merciless, hurrying Londoners! Why was I made
   For the long and painful deathbed coming to me?'

She puts her fingers in his, as, loving and silly
   At long-past Kensington dances she used to do
'It's cheaper to take the tube to Piccadilly
   And then we can catch a nineteen or twenty-two'.

MONIZA ALVI

Post-Traumatic

Not now said the mind to the brain
Not yet

And it cloaked itself in amnesia
And time curled up serpent-like –
its dusty mosaics
                              cemented together

Time – the cobra
waiting to unleash
                              its venom
Not yet, not yet

But under pressure, the mind
started to leak
                    vermilion drops

That woman jostling you in the crowd –
you could drive your fist
                              like a bus
right through her

Talk to yourself
                    Talk to yourself

You don't need to do anything

It's expected
the fuck-offs fired from your mouth

the avalanche
                of words

Until at last you made a clearing
set the house, the plot of land
in some kind of order, little
                            by little

Planted a flower
                more open-faced

which now you name
                    tentatively –
calm-in-the-storm

love-of-life

ALAN JENKINS

Launderette: Her Last Nightdress

A cotton one with a few flowers and a bit of lace
At the neck, her name-tag stitched inside, it falls
From my bag of socks and shirts and smalls
And looks so innocent, so out of place
I see her again, hot and flustered in the ward

We took her to, and helpless, late at night
When even she admitted 'something wasn't right'
And I left her waving, and she sort of smiled
To say I mustn't worry, must get on,
Get back, to sleep, to work, to my important life.

Next day, I went to M&S, I bought
The nightdress she had asked for as an afterthought
And took it in to her, and she put it on
And loved it – no more the sad, unreconciled,
Bewildered woman I had fought, no more

My father's tetchy, disappointed wife;
Girlish almost. So it was what she wore
Until one day I walked in and found her lying
In a hospital gown, so starched and plain
And straitlaced, with strings that needed tying
While this pretty one had gone into her drawer –
The something that was wrong had made a stain,
A stench I took away with me somehow
To wash, and forgot about till now
I stand here in the warm soap-smelling air

But can't remember why, and people stare.

MARIN SORESCU

Pure Pain

I don't feel ill in order to feel better,
I feel ill in order to feel worse.
Like the sea with its green, treacherous waves,
You cannot sound the bottom of pain.

I dive into pure pain,
Essence of scream and despair,
And I return to the surface blue and pale,
Like a diver who lost
His oxygen tank.

To the emperor of fishes, I beg,
Kindly send me your trustworthy shark
To cut short my passing.

translated by Adam J. Sorkin and Lidia Vianu

JO SHAPCOTT

Composition

Latent inhibition: the ability we have to filter out irrelevant stimuli

MARK LYTHGOE

And I sat among the dust motes, my pencil
(blue) sounding loud on the page, and
a blast of sun hit a puddle

and a distant radio told the news. I saw
a winter tree and then eternity trembled
and my fingers smelled of garlic from before

and the window was smeary, the tea cups
wanted washing and the Gulf Stream
was slowing and O my hips

ached from sitting. My brain's not right,
really:
its latent inhibition so way out

that even a hangnail thrilled;
I was drowning in possibility
while underneath the world

an ice shelf collapsed into the sea
and a cat with a white-tipped tail
walked by and somewhere in my body

the changed cells gathered
and my hair was damp on my neck
and I prayed to be disturbed
and hurricanoes whirled and hissed,
my nose itched, my ears hurt,
and then there was this.

from Coriolanus, I.i.

MENENIUS:

There was a time when all the body's members
Rebell'd against the belly; thus accus'd it:
That only like a gulf it did remain
I' the midst o' the body, idle and unactive,
Still cupboarding the viand, never bearing
Like labour with the rest; where the other instruments
Did see, and hear, devise, instruct, walk, feel,
And, mutually participate, did minister
Unto the appetite and affection common
Of the whole body. The belly answer'd ...

                        ... With a kind of smile,
Which ne'er came from the lungs, but even thus,
– For, look you, I may make the belly smile
As well as speak – it tauntingly replied
To the discontented members, the mutinous parts
That envied his receipt; even so most fitly
As you malign our senators for that
They are not such as you ...

                        Note me this, good friend;
Your most grave belly was deliberate,
Not rash like his accusers, and thus answer'd –
'True is it, my incorporate friends,' quoth he,
'That I receive the general food at first,
Which you do live upon; and fit it is;
Because I am the store-house, and the shop
Of the whole body: but, if you do remember,

I send it through the rivers of your blood,
Even to the court, the heart, to the seat o' the brain,
And, through the cranks and offices of man,
The strongest nerves and small inferior veins,
From me receive that natural competency
Whereby they live: and though that all at once,
You, my good friends,' – this says the belly, mark me –

       ... 'Though all at once cannot
See what I do deliver out to each:
Yet I can make my audit up, that all
From me do back receive the flour of all,
And leave me but the bran.'

SEAN O'BRIEN

The Hand

*A repeated procedure for Dupuytren's Contracture may unavoidably
result in stiffness and some loss of sensation*

My good right hand, farewell to you.
I must begin to take my leave,
And shall depart through your extremity.
I cannot hold a friend's hand now,
Nor form a fist, nor open in a wave.
They say the only remedies
For what ails me are ailments too:
They had to kill the hand they fought to save.
Lie still and let me look at you.
You seem unmoved: I am the one undone,
And so let go of you, my hand.
Although you still extend on my behalf,
Now that my grasp of you is gone
Nothing remains to comprehend.
Therefore I watch you endlessly
For your resemblance to the real,
And see the same smashed knuckle,
The scarring and the same club thumb,
The inability to feel
Made flesh, but unequipped for rage or love:
And yet you ache, as if with cold,
As armour might, remembering
Its heartlessness, its iron fist
Imprisoned in its iron glove.

GESUALDO MANZELLA-FRONTINI

The Anatomy Room

Perfumed autumn of amaryllises
acrid odor of phenic acid:
the anatomy room revealed
in the dwindling light of vesper-time all violet and gold.
Sprawled, lopsided cadavers
on stained and clotted tables.
An old man, eyes popping,
chest caved-in,
and over the jelly of his doomed eyes
the flies, unpunished,
contentedly buzzing.
Sheet of a newspaper –
the worldly note –
stuffed into the fetid mouth
of a consumptive
being measured by the deft track of the scalpel.
The sternum gives,
the bright and ruined lungs
wheeze
under pressure.
On the last table,
in shadow,
a woman split in half from the hips,
beneath the thin and rigid breasts
the belly oozing:
ah why, why, excellent creature,
surprise of my vision,

do I dandle myself before you, in the glossy whiteness
of your limbs,
a voyeur of the sudden freshness
of your vain and chaste beauty?

translated by Felix Stefanile

ROBERT LOWELL

Eye and Tooth

My whole eye was sunset red,
the old cut cornea throbbed,
I saw things darkly,
as through an unwashed goldfish globe.

I lay all day on my bed.
I chain-smoked through the night,
learning to flinch
at the flash of a matchlight.

Outside, the summer rain,
a simmer of rot and renewal,
fell in pinpricks.
Even new life is fuel.

My eyes throb.
Nothing can dislodge
the house with my first tooth
noosed in a knot to the doorknob.

Nothing can dislodge
the triangular blotch
of rot on the red roof,
a cedar hedge, or the shade of a hedge.

No ease from the eye
of the sharp-shinned hawk in the birdbook there,
with reddish-brown buffalo hair
on its shanks, one ascetic talon

clasping the abstract imperial sky.
It says:
an eye for an eye,
a tooth for a tooth.

No ease for the boy at the keyhole,
his telescope,
when the women's white bodies flashed
in the bathroom. Young, my eyes began to fail.

Nothing! No oil
for the eye, nothing to pour
on those waters or flames.
I am tired. Everyone's tired of my turmoil.

PHILIP LARKIN

Ambulances

Closed like confessionals, they thread
Loud noons of cities, giving back
None of the glances they absorb.
Light glossy grey, arms on a plaque,
They come to rest at any kerb:
All streets in time are visited.

Then children strewn on steps or road,
Or women coming from the shops
Past smells of different dinners, see
A wild white face that overtops
Red stretcher-blankets momently
As it is carried in and stowed,

And sense the solving emptiness
That lies just under all we do,
And for a second get it whole,
So permanent and blank and true.
The fastened doors recede. *Poor soul,*
They whisper at their own distress;

For borne away in deadened air
May go the sudden shut of loss
Round something nearly at an end,
And what cohered in it across
The years, the unique random blend
Of families and fashions, there

At last begin to loosen. Far
From the exchange of love to lie
Unreachable inside a room
The traffic parts to let go by
Brings closer what is left to come,
And dulls to distance all we are.

W.N. HERBERT

Revenant

Too weak to more than tap upon the wrong-paint door
   there ought to be a key that he no longer has
a shuffling in in slippers now he cannot speak
   you are a stranger in the way that seems at home
the house as was now ends upon the kitchen step
   from there on in it isn't and the back wall's skull
has opened and the names for here stepped out or fell
   a scrabble for the number at the hospital
a cardigan for four miles and his nose runs cold
   and all the sheds where he developed shots are gone
a barn-big sitting room that guts the ghosts of brick
   there is another threshold here he cannot cross
those orange washes and the violet-smeared walls
   there is a corner where the sink would like to be
the spatters of his arteries are now a matt
   he lies on varnished timber and the vanished rug
the sense of an old woman you appeased with flowers
   the nurses had to jump into a colleague's car
asperging all the bedrooms, wooden sword in hand
   he can no longer tell you how he curls there, safe
a cushion underneath his head, your own old blanket
   the nurses can't imagine how he got this far
how he regarded something through you in the walls
   the thing that you can still call home surviving much
the sense of how to get there what you don't yet know.

THOM GUNN

Memory Unsettled

Your pain still hangs in air,
Sharp motes of it suspended;
The voice of your despair –
That also is not ended:

When near your death a friend
Asked you what he could do,
'Remember me,' you said.
We will remember you.

Once when you went to see
Another with a fever
In a like hospital bed,
With terrible hothouse cough
And terrible hothouse shiver
That soaked him and then dried him,
And you perceived that he
Had to be comforted,

You climbed in there beside him
And hugged him plain in view,
Though you were sick enough,
And had your own fears too.

PHINEAS FLETCHER

from The Purple Island, or The Isle of Man
ON VEINS, ARTERIES AND NERVES

Nor is there any part in all this land,
But is a little Isle; for thousand brooks
In azure channels glide on silver sand;
Their serpent windings, and deceiving crooks
    Circling about, and wat'ring all the plain,
    Empty themselves into th'all-drinking main;
And creeping forward slide, but never turn again.

Three diff'ring streams from fountains different,
Neither in nature nor in shape agreeing,
(Yet each with other friendly ever went)
Give to this Isle his fruitfulness and being:
    The first in single channels sky-like blue,
    With luke-warm waters dyed in porphyr hue,
Sprinkle this crimson Isle with purple colour'd dew.

The next, though from the same springs first it rise,
Yet passing through another greater fountain,
Doth lose his former names and qualities:
Through many a dale it flows, and many a mountain;
    More fiery light, and needful more than all;
    And therefore fenced with a double wall,
All froths his yellow streams with many a sudding fall.

The last, in all things diff'ring from the other,
Fall from an hill, and close together go,
Embracing as they run, each with his brother;
Guarded with double trenches sure they flow:
    The coldest spring, yet nature best they have;
    And like the lacteal stones which heaven pave,
Slide down to every part with their thick milky wave.

These with a thousand streams through th'Island roving,
Bring tribute in; the first gives nourishment,
Next life, last sense and arbitrary moving:
For when the Prince hath now his mandate sent,
    The nimble posts quick down the river run,
    And end their journey, though but now begun;
But now the mandate came, and now the mandate's done.

MAURA DOOLEY

STENT!

Dearest Heart,
'felt, 'rending, 'broken,
it's what I know you by.

                        Repeat
again and again
                please repeat.

Angina Pectoris rustles her wings
and all the old familiar words
are under attack.

                Let's edit.
Let's make one tiny, precise
amendment and leave the work
as it always was, perfect.

IAN HAMILTON

Admission

The chapped lips of the uniformed night-porter
Mumble horribly against the misted glass
Of our black ambulance.
Our plight
Inspires a single, soldierly, contemptuous stare
And then he waves us on, to Blighty.

JOHN ARMSTRONG

from The Art of Preserving Health

The blood, the fountain whence the spirits flow,
The generous stream that waters every part,
And motion, vigour, and warm life conveys
To every particle that moves and lives;
This vital fluid, through unnumbered tubes
Poured by the heart, and to the heart again
Refunded; scourged for ever round and round;
Enraged with heat and toil, at last forgets
Its balmy nature: virulent and thin
It grows; and now, but that a thousand gates
Are open to its flight, it would destroy
The parts it cherished and repaired before.
Besides, the flexible and tender tubes
Melt in the mildest, most nectareous tide
That ripening Nature rolls; as in the stream
Its crumbling banks; but what the vital force
Of plastic fluids hourly batters down,
That very force, those plastic particles
Rebuild: so mutable the state of man.
For this the watchful appetite was given,
Daily with fresh materials to repair
This unavoidable expense of life,
This necessary waste of flesh and blood.
Hence the concoctive powers, with various art,
Subdue the cruder aliments to chyle;
The chyle to blood; the foamy purple tide
To liquors, which through finer arteries
To different parts their winding course pursue;
To try new changes, and new forms put on,
Or for the public, or some private use.

POLLY CLARK

Cheng du Massage

I lie tidy as an English village
while her fingers sting me with sleet,
her snowball fists smash into me.
She pads around me, light as a coot,
before hammering exploding nails
into my thighs – then on to my temples,
pressing till my eyes spark –
and I see nothing but China's
electric bones, its face of fog –
and my own giant muteness, piled and blind,
unlovely and stubborn as cement.

FRED D'AGUIAR

Obeah Mama Dot
(her remedies)

I
I am knotted in pain.
She measures string
From navel to each nipple.

She kneads into my belly
Driving the devil
Out of my enforced fast.

II
For the fevers to subside,
I must drink the bush
Boiled to a green alluvium,

In one headback slake;
And return to bouncing around,
Side-stepping bushes for days.

III
A head-knock mushrooms
Into a bold, bald,
Softened bulb.

Her poultice filled
At the end of a rainbow –
The sun above Kilimanjaro;

The murderous vial drawn,
Till the watery mound
Is a crater in burnt ground.

IV
Our rocking-chair counsellor:
Her words untangling us
from bramble and plimpler notions

Into this sudden miles-clearing.

PAUL MULDOON

The Birth

Seven o'clock. The seventh day of the seventh month of the year.
No sooner have I got myself up in lime-green scrubs,
a sterile cap and mask,
and taken my place at the head of the table

than the windlass-women ply their shears
and gralloch-grub
for a footling foot, then, warming to their task,
haul into the inestimable

realm of apple-blossoms and chanterelles and damsons and eel-
    spears
and foxes and the general hubbub
of inkies and jennets and Kickapoos with their lemniscs
or peekaboo-quiffs of Russian sable

and tallow-unctuous vernix, into the realm of the widgeon –
the 'whew' or 'yellow-poll', not the 'zuizin' –

Dorothy Aoife Korelitz Muldoon: I watch through floods of tears
as they give her a quick rub-a-dub
and whisk
her off to the nursery, then check their staple-guns for staples.

WILLIAM CARLOS WILLIAMS

The World Contracted to a Recognizable Image

at the small end of an illness
there was a picture
probably Japanese
which filled my eye

an idiotic picture
except it was all I recognised
the wall lived for me in that picture
I clung to it as to a fly

PIA TAFDRUP

Blood Seconds

Drops of blood burn their way through the snow
with their salt crystal, an opening, a depth of light,
a space that expands without resistance.
Close to is what seems near,
far away: A shot, fleeting fiery colours,
stripes of blood that steaming lead into the forest
where the hunter cannot find the wounded animal,
before the darkness falls, but returns
and is stopped on the path, spitefully stared at by the blind cat.

Blood warms the winter, melts blocks of ice,
the blood in the animal, the blood in the person,
the circling blood of family and friendships.
The heart's prism, the veins' tracery and branchings
in a constant murmur: Why are we here?
What do we want? Where are we going?
Drop-fall. Blood seconds counted by a star,
the body's water is the blood that smells red,
waves that rise in a regulated chaos.

Blood is the present, the time of desire,
the warm touch and the time of blessing.
A horizon of roses planted for the night,
an odour of iron sticks to the sex,
the woman's blood, pure as an unwritten sheet.
There are two kinds of women: Those who swallow
the semen, and those who spit it out –
And there are two kinds of men: Those who lick
a bleeding woman, and those who don't –

The time of fire, the time of earth, the time of air,
the time of blood and water, the time of lovers,
a purling spring, a ceaseless motion.
Taught by an older sister the young girl washes her clothes
in cold water, and it is not a fairytale.
The pulse is counted, world seconds are counted:
The time of fire, the time of earth, the time of air,
the time of blood and persecutions, names
hurled out into frost-cold air are enumerated, one by one.

Countries' borders are not moved with rivers of blood,
just as cities are not built from spilt blood,
blood merely opens the earth's crust to seep down
and only enemies are consoled by blood.
The time of hatred or judgement,
the blood that flows to the final sleep.
An unexpected plummeting of birds, a celestial cobweb
of threads that break, the time of death –
or the light's pale membranes penetrated?

                              translated by David McDuff

CHARLES SIMIC

Hotel Insomnia

I liked my little hole,
Its window facing a brick wall.
Next day there was a piano.
A few evenings a month
A crippled old man came to play
'My Blue Heaven'.

Mostly, though, it was quiet.
Each room with its spider in heavy overcoat
Catching his fly with a web
Of cigarette smoke and revery.
So dark,
I could not see my face in the shaving mirror.

At 5 a.m. the sound of bare feet upstairs.
The 'Gypsy' fortune-teller,
Whose storefront is on the corner,
Going to pee after a night of love.
Once, too, the sound of a child sobbing.
So near it was, I thought
For a moment, I was sobbing myself.

RAINER MARIA RILKE

Going Blind

She sat just like the others at the table.
But on second glance, she seemed to hold her cup
a little differently as she picked it up.
She smiled once. It was almost painful.

And when they finished and it was time to stand
and slowly, as chance selected them, they left
and moved through many rooms (they talked and laughed),
I saw her. She was moving far behind

the others, absorbed, like someone who will soon
have to sing before a large assembly;
upon her eyes, which were radiant with joy,
light played as on the surface of a pool.

She followed slowly, taking a long time,
as though there were some obstacle in the way;
and yet: as though, once it was overcome,
she would be beyond all walking, and would fly.

translated by Stephen Mitchell

CAITRÍONA O'REILLY

Thin

It is chill and dark in my small room.
A wind blows through gaps in the roof,
piercing even the eiderdown. My skin
goose-pimples in front of the cloudy glass
though there was scalding tea for dinner
with an apple. I'm cold to the bone.

I don't sleep well either. My hip-bones
stick in the foam mattress, and the room's
so empty. My sister is having dinner
with a boy. Awake under the roof
I watch the stars bloom heavily through glass
and think, *how shatterproof is my skin?*

I doze till six, then drink semi-skim
milk for breakfast (the bare bones
of a meal) before nine o'clock class.
It's kind of hard to leave my room
for the walk to school. No roof
over me, and eight solid hours till dinner-

time. All day my dreams of dinner
are what really get under my skin,
not the boys. My tongue sticks to the roof
of my mouth again in class. I'm such a bone-
head! And my stomach's an empty room.
My face floats upwards in a glass

of Coke at lunchtime. One glass.
I make it last the whole day till dinner:
hot tea and an apple in my room.
My sister seems not to notice the skin
around my mouth or my ankle bones.
If our parents knew they'd hit the roof

I suppose. My ribs rise like the roof
of a house that's fashioned from glass.
I might even ping delicately like bone-
china when flicked. No dinner
for six weeks has made this skin
more habitable, more like a room –

or a ceiling that shatters like glass
over those diners off gristle and bone.
This skin is a more distinguished room.

Booking Khan Singh Kumar

Must I wear only masks that don't sit for a Brit
Would you blush if I stripped from my native skin

Should I beat on my chest I'm a ghetto poet
Who discorded his kind as they couldn't know it

Should I foot it featly as a Punjab in Punglish
Sold on an island wrecked by the British

Did *you* make me for the gap in the market
Did *I* make me for the gap in the market

Does it feel groovy in the gap in the market
Does it get gooey in the gap in the market ...

Will I flame on the tree that your canon has stoked
Will I thistle at the bole where a bull dog has cocked

Should I talk with the chalk of my white inside
On the board of my minstrel – blacked outside

Should I bleach my bile-name or mash it to a stink
Should I read for you straight or Gunga Din this gig

Did *you* make me for the gap in the market
Did *I* make me for the gap in the market

Does it feel groovy in the gap in the market
Does it get gooey in the gap in the market ...

As I've worn a sari bride and an English Rose
Can I cream off awards from your melting pot phase

Do you medal yourselves when you meddle with my type
If I go up di spectrum how far can ju dye

More than your shell-like, your clack applause
What bothers is whether you'll boo me off the face if I balls

Out of Indian!

Natural Causes

On the very day that our boy was born
– the very same morning, in fact –
I left him beside his mother,
drove dizzily out of the hospital,
stopped at a grille-covered shop,
bought my paper, went home, and read –
after I'd shaved and bathed and dozed
for an hour or two in a stupor of joy –
the story of how an amusing, clever,
and now inconsolable man was one day
leading a more or less blameless life,
and the next day went crazy with fear.

He thought he was getting the flu.
He was put to bed, and four days later
escaped to be found in a cab
by his terrified wife, unable to think
what his address might be, or his name.
The hospital then, and every day since –
to discover his memory worked
just well enough to remind him
his memory no longer worked.
Give him the washing up: no trouble –
each plate that he takes is the first.
Give him a long afternoon to sleep
in the sun-strewn hospital grounds,
and every three seconds he'll wake
to his utterly fresh despair.

Our son is a month old today,
and to celebrate woke us at 5 a.m.,

of course. A dingy, rain-spattered dawn,
and the three of us lay in our big double bed
with the pig in the middle between us feeding
with slobbery, wheezy, chirruping grunts.
Because it was early, because I was tired,
because I was almost lost to the world
with love for the boy, the thought of the man
with no memory came to me – as it had come,
I should say, hundreds of times before –
nervously, slithering into my mind
like a dog on a heavy painful rope,
yet lazily too, like a dog on a dusty day,
and stopped there: sinewy, not to be argued with,
bitter, but somehow banal, dragging behind it
other thoughts: *Those whom the gods ...*
In the midst of life ... The Lord taketh away ...
What do we do to deserve ... that sort of thing.

I've told you already, it's come to me
hundreds of times, the thought of the stranger
prowling his tucked-away hospital room –
which means I've encountered him often
each day in the life of our boy,
trying to compensate one with the other,
yet never quite able to bring them together,
except in a picture which hinges itself
in a triptych: the stranger on one side
stuck in a room with a single dazzling bulb,
who sees death laying its hand on his head
over and over again; in the centre, our boy,
a bundle shoved out to sea in one of those
hopeless wickerwork coracles under a furious sky;
and lastly ourselves – intelligent, petrified,
no way out of a cupboard of shiny steel with walls
which steadily squeeze together until we die.

SARAH MAGUIRE

May Day, 1986

for Tadeusz Sławek

Yesterday, the weather in Warsaw
was the same as London's: *Sunny, 18°*
(sixty-four Fahrenheit). I am sitting
in a walled garden drinking gin,
the fading sky as blue as this tonic water
loosening its bubbles against the flat ice.

What is in the air? The first midges;
a television three doors down, its hum
like this lone bat avoiding the walnut tree.
A dog barks. In other houses lights come on –
the street an Advent Calendar opening
its doors. This house is in darkness,

its seven windows admitting the night.
I'm trying to read *Mansfield Park*, to learn
how Fanny finds love and a mansion
through keeping silence. All week
the weather report has plotted the wind
leaving Chernobyl with its freight

of fall-out: cancer settling on Poland –
the radio-activity an inaudible fizz
in the cells, rupturing thorax or liver,
the intimacy of the bowel. They say it won't
reach here. I stare at the sky till all
I can see are the dead cells of my eyes,

jumping and falling. It's too dark to read –
only the flare of a late *Kerria japonica*,
trained to the wall. I think of your letter
in my drawer with the handkerchiefs,
one page torn by an earlier reader. Socrates
distrusted writing, its distance from

the grain of the voice. I come indoors
to write you all the things I couldn't say
a year ago. Later, on the news, they will show
gallons of contaminated Polish milk
swilled into sewage, a boy crying
at the sting of iodine he must swallow

against the uncertain air.

ROBERT LOWELL

Home After Three Months Away

Gone now the baby's nurse,
a lioness who ruled the roost
and made the Mother cry.
She used to tie
gobbets of porkrind in bowknots of gauze –
three months they hung like soggy toast
on our eight foot magnolia tree,
and helped the English sparrows
weather a Boston winter.

Three months, three months!
Is Richard now himself again?
Dimpled with exaltation,
my daughter holds her levee in the tub.
Our noses rub –
each of us pats a stringy lock of hair –
they tell me nothing's gone.
Though I am forty-one,
not forty now, the time I put away
was child's play. After thirteen weeks
my child still dabs her cheeks
to start me shaving. When
we dress her in her sky-blue corduroy,
she changes to a boy,
and floats my shaving brush
and washcloth in the flush ...
Dearest, I cannot loiter here
in lather, like a polar bear.

Recuperating, I neither spin nor toil.
Three stories down below,
a choreman tends our coffin's length of soil,
and seven horizontal tulips blow.
Just twelve months ago,
these flowers were pedigreed
imported Dutchmen, now no one need
distinguish them from weed.
Bushed by the late spring snow,
they cannot meet
another year's snowballing enervation.

I keep no rank nor station.
Cured, I am frizzled, stale and small.

MICHAEL LASKEY

Early Morning Waking

He turns towards the door, the rattle
of a trolley or a bed pushed past –
not for him, not till after breakfast
which he won't get, seeing he's nil
      by mouth.

And he's hungry now, sick for home,
for a normal school morning – Joe nicking
the last of the milk, deadly flicking
with the tea towel, Sal texting Simone,
      hot toast.

Then the rush for the bus, he stands out
in the drizzle with Tom, won't shiver
against the post office wall with the others,
those girls. Tom brought him the hand-outs
      at first.

French irregular verbs for a test
next Monday, with another test due
that he can't bunk off or scrape through
by mugging up stuff at the last
      minute.

But he won't think of that, he rolls over
and lies on his back, a log floating
down river, slowly spinning, hoping
not to snag, to drift off, recover
      the knack.

Let him doze at least for the present
if he can. Soon the surgeon will remove
half his scrotum, which should improve
the prognosis, provided it isn't
                    too late.

Now the waiting. He's fifteen. Not a story
I've had to make up. Any moment you care
to pick contains him. His thick dark hair
will grow back. There won't be much more
                    chemo

with luck. The new shift's cranking up.
Someone passing laughs, maybe a nurse
going off duty. Is it any possible use
to him, to them all, my waking up
                    early?

STEPHEN KNIGHT

The Nightingale Standard

A sick person who fears his nurse or who knows that her handling of him
will cause him pain [...] is liable to get nervous and morbid.

The Family Physician, 1951

An ideal sickroom, facing west:
Ornaments and useless furnishings dispensed with,
Dusted, disinfected pictures on the wall,
Drugs placed carefully in drawers,
Light literature,
My correspondence littering the floor,
Damp dusters for the woodwork,
Beef tea, soon.

Now, I'm drinking cocoa from the nibs.
Clear, like coffee, and most refreshing. Refreshing me.
Wine whey? Milk tea? Egg flip?
– Please. Anything but cocoa from the nibs.

Business-like in rubber heels, methodical,
Nurse contemplates the muscles of my face.

> *Air hunger*
> *Air passages, obstruction of*
> *Alkalis*
> *Allotments*
> *Amputation*
> *Anvil bone*

Stewed according to size and age,
Stewed pigeon next. The trussing string
Removed, it's almost free from grease.
Broiled chops? Stewed sweetbread? Tripe?
– All right. This bird is not restoring me.

18 breaths a minute, 15 when I'm old.

A regular exchange of air:
The bottom sash raised every day;
At night, the top 3 inches.

A slight touch here, the smoothing of a wrinkle there.
The under mackintosh pulled straight.
I ruffle my covers, adopt all sorts of attitudes.
(A benefit, both mentally and physically.)

Business-like in rubber heels, methodical,
Nurse

- keeps back the crowd
- lays, around the bed, linoleum
- dashes water on my face
- applies a little powdered starch
- encourages the bleeding
- gives me ice to suck

Lathered, several times a day, with tarry soap,
I'm trussed from toe to head.

18 breaths a minute, 15 when I'm old.

Looking for the bottle labelled POISON,
Nurse shows her strength of character.
She has given me a sporting chance.

I have no foreign bodies in my feet.
I have no fish hook in my hand.

> *Russell viper*
> *Rubber bandages*
> *Robert Jones abduction frame*
> *Roundworm*
> *Rigor mortis*
> *Rickety rosary*
> *Reticulitis*
> Rescue me

SELIMA HILL

Nothing

Because she is exhausted
and confused,

and doesn't want to argue,
and can't speak,

she dreams of nothing
for a thousand years,

or what the nurses cheerfully call
a week.

ZBIGNIEW HERBERT

The Hygiene of the Soul

We live in the narrow bed of our flesh. Only the inexperienced twist in it without interruption. Rotating around one's own axis is not allowed because then sharp threads wind themselves on to the heart as on to a spool.

It is necessary to fold one's hands behind the neck, half-shut the eyes and float down that lazy river, from the Fount of the Hair as far as the first Cataract of the Great Toenail.

translated by Czeslaw Milosz and Peter Dale Scott

EMILY DICKINSON

'My first well Day – since many ill –'

My first well Day – since many ill –
I asked to go abroad –
And take the Sunshine in my hands,
And see the things in Pod –

A blossom just when I went in
To take my Chance with pain –
Uncertain if myself, or He,
Should prove the strongest One.

The Summer deepened, while we strove –
She put some flowers away –
And Redder cheeked Ones – in their stead –
A fond – illusive way –

To cheat Herself, it seemed she tried –
As if before a child
To fade – Tomorrow – Rainbows held
The Sepulchre, could hide.

She dealt a fashion to the Nut –
She tied the Hoods to Seeds –
She dropped bright scraps of Tint, about –
And left Brazilian Threads

On every shoulder that she met –
Then both her Hands of Haze
Put up – to hide her parting Grace
From our unfitted eyes.

My loss, by sickness – Was it Loss?
Or that Ethereal Gain
One earns by measuring the Grave –
Then – measuring the Sun –

WILLIAM COWPER

Lines Written During a Period of Insanity

Hatred and vengeance, my eternal portion,
Scarce can endure delay of execution,
Wait, with impatient readiness, to seize my
                        Soul in a moment.

Damn'd below Judas: more abhorr'd than he was,
Who for a few pence sold his holy Master.
Twice betrayed Jesus me, the last delinquent,
                        Deems the profanest.

Man disavows, and Deity disowns me:
Hell might afford my miseries a shelter;
Therefore hell keeps her ever hungry mouths all
                        Bolted against me.

Hard lot! encompass'd with a thousand dangers;
Weary, faint, trembling with a thousand terrors;
I'm called, if vanquish'd, to receive a sentence
                        Worse than Abiram's.

Him the vindictive rod of angry justice
Sent quick and howling to the centre headlong;
I, fed with judgment, in a fleshly tomb, am
                        Buried above ground.

IAN HAMILTON

Awakening

Your head, so sick, is leaning against mine,
So sensible. You can't remember
Why you're here, nor do you recognize
These helping hands.
My love,
The world encircles us. We're losing ground.

Want

The more you look the more remote
I am to you not as a star but a stone

kicked to the edge of a lane two roads in
from the sea in a dead-end town.

You won't think to look there.
Because you're here

in this bright room, bent over the blur
of threads that's led you here where

you daren't move for fear of upsetting
whatever it is that's stopping you getting

what you want – a tower
of fine bone china

in a dark corner,
growing higher and higher;

here where you come closest to me,
me who is really you – you

as small, knuckled want,
impotent, clean, clock-watching want.

But you know how it is.
I'll come to you when you're a mess,

pissed probably, putting it about,
when you've loosed yourself from the thought

of yourself and world crashes in with its crowds
of stricken infants, its mad array of flowers.

O oestrogen, astrology, buseralin and cells,
HCG, Day 14, the transmigration of souls!

It's all more or less than you could ever know.
So stop, little no-mother. Come outside. Throw

yourself back onto a strong wind;
take in the sky, hold on to nothing.

GERARD WOODWARD

Dr Profundo

I shouldn't have looked into his eyes
But somehow they just drew me in.
That's how I was hypnotised.

His services were advertised –
Does your memory sometimes let you down?
I shouldn't have looked into his eyes.

I'd thought it was a pack of lies,
I'd thought he was a charlatan.
That's how I was hypnotised.

And the memories came like butterflies
Across the meadows of my brain,
I shouldn't have looked into his eyes,

And seen my life so summarised,
Every error and every sin,
That's how I was hypnotised.

And now I want it all revised,
It's hell recalling everything
I shouldn't have looked into his eyes,
That's how I was hypnotised.

C.K. WILLIAMS

Of Childhood the Dark: *Danger*

Watch out, you might fall, as that one fell,
or fall *ill*, as he or she did, or die,

or worse, not die, be insufficient,
less than what should be your worth.

Be cautious of your body, which isn't you,
though neither are you its precise other;

you're what it feels, and the knowing
what's felt, yet no longer quite either.

Your life is first of all what may be lost,
its ultimate end not to end.

ANN SANSOM

On Psoriasis

Question upon question may be asked – the disease is capricious
and refuses to part with its innermost secret.

G. LOMHOLT

This is neither
Updike's mansion of hidden delights,
nor Potter's bombsite. Neither is it
Nabokov's safe house. Nevertheless

a lamp blooms in each window,
and every gable glows, red on white.
Strings of bulbs bud, unlit, in the trees.

The drive is a miracle of alarms, sensors.
There is no point in caution.

*

Every hallway
is an invitation; this is yours.
Give me your hand,
the raw artwork of your condition.
Can you believe
I won't recoil?

*

This is the house
where flesh once entered flesh, rejoiced
in giving all it has, in opening
at last to life, the delight
in opening a door
to the dust
you now brush off your coat.

*

Let me take your coat.
Once I would have asked
Is the skin of your flesh a rising, a scab?
So that – feared like leprosy –
you might be judged; absolved
or driven out. Only the innocent
were healed entirely; the blind
restored, the lame made whole,
the dead raised. You
might have been cleansed.
Conditionally.

*

Now I can offer
anointments, unguents,
bright booths, baths slick
with mercury, gold or lime,
goggles for the ice-green eyes
of the sloughing serpent.

*

Bats are waking in a closed room,
wasps jostle in a cavity;
they practise a perpetual tune,
waiting. Only we can hear them

*

Look out across
the warm night harbour, a breeze
quenches the small lights, briefly.
And, after snowfall, the valley
knows its rubble soothed for hours.
What is ingrained will surface,
weeping. But there are times of reprieve.

*

Yes. And cinders shift and settle
in the grate, a drizzle of ash to the hearth
where you warm your back.
There are nights you can unpick
the whole thing; open the scalp across,
grip two-handed, draw down the face.
Time's only mercy is the release of skin
from bone; dividing what's bred in, what's shown.
And so your face falls, disappointed,
as if it were meant to fit a larger skull.
And this persistence, nothing but a song
in celebration of exuberance,
a song sung out of tune, too fast

*

So ease what is now
a gown, off one elbow,
the other,
then, in a storm of scurf,
wriggle it a damp unresistant bag
from the chest, the twin mask
of the nipples, then
without regret
fast over belly hips
the knot that bound us
the cleft that fired us
the cock that defined us

raw now but painless
the thighs, crouched, a moment
when it's easier to say Yes,
to reach down and ease the calves,
from each arched foot, old socks

you may step out of, yes,
and kick away, not stumbling.
Will you dance at last?

*

Still, we can no more flay ourselves
than we can be reborn. Sometimes
we can rest. We can, invited in,
take possesssion of a house, wait
like guests in the hallway
for the healing question
coming something like an itch.

FRANK O'HARA

Anxiety

I'm having a real day of it.
　　　　　　　　　　There was
something I had to do. But what?
There are no alternatives, just
the one something.
　　　　　　　　I have a drink,
it doesn't help – far from it!
　　　　　　　　　　　I
feel worse. I can't remember how
I felt, so perhaps I feel better.
No. Just a little darker.
　　　　　　　　　　If I could
get really dark, richly dark, like
being drunk, that's the best that's
open as a field. Not the best,

but the best except for the impossible
pure light, to be as if above a vast
prairie, rushing and pausing over
the tiny golden heads in deep grass.

But still now, familiar laughter low
from a dark face, affection human and often even –
motivational? the warm walking night
　　　　　　　　　　　　wandering
amusement of darkness, lips,
　　　　　　　　and
the light, always in wind. Perhaps
that's it: to clean something. A window?

GWYNETH LEWIS

Glaucoma

Glaucoma won't let my mother knit:
fine wool is a problem, her most intricate stitch

no longer viable. Unravelling doesn't require sight.
Look into her eyeball and you'll see light

receptors twinkling like stars. Ganglion cells die,
darken the supernovae,

lovely eclipses for others to see
in our intimate, sighted jelly.

On the coast, each village had a different style
of fisherman's sweater, they say. The tide

reads blackberry stitch like Braille
with dexterous pressure, untangling the wool

of tendons. Tears are a retreating sea
full of dark fish swimming. Knit one, purl three.

CHERYL FOLLON

Madam Aphrodisia

A cup of cocoa was never so much fun!
    But don't look so nervous –
        you too can act like Casanova!
        And I have all the answers!
    Or how six hundred women were serviced
by the one big appetite of an African king!

It's thought that caraway seeds assist the digestion,
    but they're part of the lovers' cult
        so use them in your cooking!
        The bed-frame's furious rocking
    will be one result
and a lover who will humour any suggestion.

Three gull eggs from Mullingar
    neatly broken over
        a mixture of honey and ginger
        and spread on the cock of your lover
    should keep him loving deeper,
longer. Enjoy this little gift of pleasure.

A diet of fennel, lentils, peas and beans,
    washed down with a little wine
        will have you in top shape –
        you've never seen it stand so straight!
    And the strength of two men!
Mark how your delighted lady screams!

Forget the peacock tongues of ancient Rome.
    Try a single onion
        baked with butter and ginger
        and scrape of nutmeg for good measure.
    That's sure to get you going –
even Rome didn't know such hedonism!

The lands of hashish, strange roots and fasting –
    I have seen them all –
        China, India, Asia
        and know their importance to lovers
    who want to give their all.
Try cherries mixed with milk for lasting passion.

You have bought my wares, wise woman –
    the delicate white powder
        dusting your big tits
        will have him standing straight and stiff
    for hours on end, and longer!
Let nature work for you in rose and jasmine.

At one time Egyptian monks were bound
    never to eat fish.
        Perhaps it was just as well,
        as when members start to swell
    while partaking of Venus's gifts,
when would any sacred work get done?

A man who took a magpie's egg in the morning
    raw and on its own
        to boost his sexual prowess,
        said his wife was always late to dress.
    Yes. While he vomited in the pan!
Trust my wide knowledge and heed my warnings!

I've heard that rich women and men in China
    favour the musk of a deer –
        the gland under its tail
        pumped into a glass vial!
    It's a heavy price to bear –
costing as much as gold, frankincense or myrrh!

I have a special root, quite like ginseng,
    powerful, when mixed,
        so it's more of a personal recipe –
        but I warn you, use sparingly.
    There is nothing worse
than fading too soon from the heart of the action!

A ring of straw! An amulet of teeth!
    What good are they?
        You must beware of cranks
        spoiling love-play with pranks –
    but not my array –
they're sure to leave you joyful and out of breath!

IAN DUHIG

From the Plague Journal

I have been asked to write about our food.

I remember nights spent hulling ration-rice,
soya beans pressed dry before they got to us,
boiling black-market sweetfish to hide their smell
from our Neighbourhood Monitor. We ate everything;
reed-root, pigweed, tugwort, bar-weed –
these may not be the scientific names.
We smuggled grated radish and bracken-sprouts
past our Neighbourhood Monitor once he started fainting,
propped beneath his Government banderols:
        'There's Always Space to Plant a Pumpkin!'
        'The War is Only Just Beginning!'

Later our food became medicine:
dried fig-grubs for the incontinence;
ant-lions in sake for the headaches;
leek-leaves and cucumber for the burns.
I sold my son's thousand-stitch belt
for peaches and eggs which I mashed and strained,
mashed and strained. Still my children died,
the last little Tadashi setting his weasel-traps
of bamboo and abalone shells round the pond
he'd stocked with a few tiny carp fry.

That is all I remember about our food.

from The Canterbury Tales:
General Prologue

    With us ther was a DOCTOUR OF PHISIK;
In al this world ne was ther noon hym lik,
To speak of phisik and of surgerye,
For he was grounded in astronomye.
He kept his patient a ful greet deel
In houres by his magyk natureel.
Wel koude he fortunen the ascendent
Of his ymages for his pacient.
He knew the cause of everich maladye,
Were it of hoot, or coold, or moyste, or drye,
And where they engendred, and of what humour.
He was a verray, parfit praktisour:
The cause yknowe, and of his harm the roote,
Anon he haf the sik man his boote.
Ful reddy hadde he his apothecaries
To sende hym drogges and his letuaries,
For ech of hem made oother for to wynne –
Hir frendshipe nas nat newe to bigynne.
Wel knew he the old Esculapius,
And Deyscorides, and eek Rufus,
Old Ypocras, Haly, and Galyen,
Serapion, Razis, and Avycen,
Averrois, Damascien, and Constantyn,
Bernard, and Gatesden, and Gilbertyn.
Of his diete mesurable was he,
For it was of no superfluitee,
But of greet norissyng and digestible.
His studie was but little on the Bible.

In sangwyn and in pers he clad was al,
Lyned with taffeta and with sendal.
And yet he was but esy of dispence;
He kepte that he wan in pestilence.
For gold in phisik is a cordial,
Therefore he lovede gold in special.

astronomie, *astrology*; magyk natureel, *science*; boote, *remedy*; letuaries,
medicinal mixtures; wynne, *profit*; Esculapius to Gilbertyn, *medical
authorities*; sangwyn, *red*; pers, *blue-grey*; sendal, *a kind of silk*; esy of
dispence, *careful in spending*; wan, *gained*; cordial, *medicine for the heart*

JAMES WRIGHT

Chilblain

My uncle Willy with his long lecherous face
Once told me wisely:
Over in France in them cathouses
In the big war,
They used to sell a salve,
That you squeezed on the inside
Of your forefinger knuckle,
And it spread all over.
Sure, it didn't cure chilblain.
But it stung so bad it took
Your mind off your troubles.
He snickered darkly, without sound,
The proud man's wisdom.
Willy the liar is buried in Colrain,
And every time in dreams I see him there
The violets and snowflakes run
Together, till all June
Earth smokes like slag.
Violets and snowflakes gather, gather
In a mock caress,
And Willy's stone clenches shut like a young man's hand
Frightened of France and winter.
Before I wake, the stone remembers
Where it is, where Ohio is,
Where violets last only a little.
Mill-smoke kills them halfway through spring,
And chilblain still stings
In June when earth smokes like slag.

LES MURRAY

It Allows a Portrait in Line Scan at Fifteen

He retains a slight 'Martian' accent, from the years of single phrases.
He no longer hugs to disarm. It is gradually allowing him affection.
It does not allow proportion. Distress is absolute, shrieking and
    runs him at frantic speed through crashing doors.
He likes cyborgs. Their taciturn power, with his intonation.
It still runs him around the house, alone in the dark, cooing and
    laughing.
He can read about soils, populations and New Zealand. On neutral
    topics he's illiterate.
Arnie Schwarzenegger is an actor. He isn't a cyborg really, is he, Dad?
He lives on forty acres, with animals and trees, and used to draw it
    continually.
He knows the map of Earth's fertile soils, and can draw it freehand.
He can only lie in a panicked shout *SorrySorryIdidn'tdoit!* warding
    off conflict with others and himself.
When he ran away constantly it was to the greengrocers to worship
    stacked fruit.
His favourite country was the Ukraine: it is nearly all deep fertile
    soil.
Giggling, he climbed all over the dim Freudian psychiatrist who
    told us how autism resulted from 'refrigerator' parents.
When asked to smile, he photographs a rictus-smile on his face.
It long forbade all naturalistic films. They were Adult movies.
If they (that is, he) *are bad the police will put them in hospital.*
He sometimes drew the farm amid Chinese or Balinese rice terraces.
When a runaway, he made uproar in the police station, playing at
    three times adult speed.
Only animated films were proper. *Who Framed Roger Rabbit* then
    authorised the rest.
Phrases spoken to him he would take as teaching, and repeat.

When he worshipped fruit, he screamed as if poisoned when it
     was fed to him.

A one-word first conversation: *Blane. – Yes! Plane, that's right, baby!*
     – Blane.

He has forgotten nothing, and remembers the precise quality of
     experiences.

It requires rulings: *Is stealing very playing up, as bad as murder?*

He counts at a glance, not looking. And he has never been lost.

When he ate only nuts and dried fruit, words were for dire
     emergencies.

He knows all the breeds of fowls, and the counties of Ireland.

He'd begun to talk, then returned to babble, then silence. It
     withdrew speech for years.

Is that very autistic, to play video games in the day?

He is anger's mirror, and magnifies any near him, raging it down.

It still won't allow him fresh fruit, or orange juice with bits in it.

He swam in the midwinter dam at night. It had no rules about cold.

He was terrified of thunder and finally cried as if in explanation
     It – angry!

He grilled an egg he'd broken into bread. Exchanges of soil-
     knowledge are called landtalking.

He lives in objectivity. I was sure Bell's palsy would leave my face
     only when he said it had begun to.

Don't say word! when he was eight forbade the word 'autistic' in
     his presence.

Bantering questions about girlfriends cause a terrified look and
     blocked ears.

He sometimes centred the farm in a furrowed American midwest.

Eye contact, Mum! means he truly wants attention. It dislikes
     I-contact.

He is equitable and kind, and only ever a little jealous. It was a
     relief when that little arrived.

He surfs, bowls, walks for miles. For many years he hasn't trailed
     his left arm while running.

I gotta get smart! looking terrified into the years. *I gotta get smart!*

JACKIE KAY

Dance of the Cherry Blossom

Both of us are getting worse
Neither knows who had it first

He thinks I gave it to him
I think he gave it to me

Nights chasing clues where
One memory runs into another like dye.

Both of us are getting worse
I know I'm wasting precious time

But who did he meet between
May 87 and March 89.

I feel his breath on my neck
A slow climb into himself then out.

In the morning it all seems different
Neither knows who had it first

We eat breakfast together – newspapers
And silence except for the slow slurp of tea

This companionship is better than anything
He thinks I gave it to him.

By lunchtime we're fighting over some petty thing
He tells me I've lost my sense of humour

I tell him I'm not Glaswegian
You all think death is a joke

It's not funny. I'm dying for fuck's sake
I think he gave it to me.

Just think he says it's every couple's dream
I won't have to wait for you up there

I'll have you night after night – your glorious legs
Your strong hard belly, your kissable cheeks

I cry when he says things like that
My shoulders cave in, my breathing trapped

Do you think you have a corner on dying
You self-pitying wretch, pathetic queen.

He pushes me; we roll on the floor like whirlwind;
When we are done in, our lips find each other

We touch soft as breeze, caress the small parts
Rocking back and forth, his arms become mine

There's nothing outside but the noise of the wind
The cherry blossom's dance through the night.

DOUGLAS DUNN

Thirteen Steps and the Thirteenth of March

She sat up on her pillows, receiving guests.
I brought them tea or sherry like a butler,
Up and down the thirteen steps from my pantry.
I was running out of vases.

More than one visitor came down, and said,
'Her room's so cheerful. She isn't afraid.'
Even the cyclamen and lilies were listening,
Their trusty tributes holding off the real.

Doorbells, shopping, laundry, post and callers,
And twenty-six steps up the stairs
From door to bed, two times thirteen's
Unlucky numeral in my high house.

And visitors, three, four, five times a day;
My wept exhaustions over plates and cups
Drained my self-pity in these days of grief
Before the grief. Flowers, and no vases left.

Tea, sherry, biscuits, cake, and whisky for the weak ...
She fought death with an understated mischief –
'I suppose I'll have to make an effort' –
Turning down painkillers for lucidity.

Some sat downstairs with a hankie
Nursing a little cry before going up to her.
They came back with their fears of dying amended.

'Her room's so cheerful. She isn't afraid.'
Each day was duty round the clock.
Our kissing conversations kept me going,
Those times together with the phone switched off,
Remembering our lives by candlelight.

John and Stuart brought their pictures round,
A travelling exhibition. Dying,
She thumbed down some, nodded at others,
An artist and curator to the last,

Honesty at all costs. She drew up lists,
Bequests, gave things away. It tore my heart out.
Her friends assisted at this tidying
In a conspiracy of women.

At night, I lay beside her in the unique hours.
There were mysteries in candle-shadows,
Birds, aeroplanes, the rabbits of our fingers,
The lovely, erotic flame of the candlelight.

Sad? Yes. But it was beautiful also.
There was a stillness in the world. Time was out
Walking his dog by the low walls and privet.
There was anonymity in words and music.

She wanted me to wear her wedding ring.
It wouldn't fit even my little finger.
It jammed on the knuckle. I knew why.
Her fingers dwindled and her rings slipped off.

After the funeral, I had them to tea and sherry
At the Newland Park. They said it was thoughtful.
I thought it was ironic – one last time –
A mad reprisal for their loyalty.

SUSAN WICKS

Optician

His pencil of light
draws me the bare branches
of my eye's blood,
sap rising in darkness
deep under the lid.

A frieze of trees repeating
on my wall of red –
the shades I lost,
painted by touch,
blaze under his torch.

Now the light is out
but the lines wait –
my deer and bison running
in their red cave.
The fire they outlive.

C.K. WILLIAMS

Dissections

Not only have the skin and flesh and parts of the skeleton
of one of the anatomical effigies in the *Musée de l'Homme*
been excised, stripped away, so that you don't look just at,
but through the thing – pink lungs, red kidney and heart,
tangles of yellowish nerves he seems snarled in, like a net;

not only are his eyes without eyelids, and so shallowly
embedded beneath the blade of the brow, that they seem,
with no shadow to modulate them, flung open in pain or fear;
and not only is his gaze so frenziedly focused that he seems to be
receiving everything, even our regard scraping across him as *blare*;

not only that, but looking more closely, I saw he was real,
that he'd been constructed, reconstructed, on an actual skeleton:
the nerves and organs were wire and plaster, but the armature,
the staring skull, the spine and ribs, were varnished, oxidising bone;
someone was there, his personhood discernible, a self, a soul.

I felt embarrassed, as though I'd intruded on someone's loneliness,
or grief, and then, I don't know why, it came to me to pray,
though I don't pray, I've unlearned how, to whom, or what,
what fiction, what illusion, or, it wouldn't matter, what true thing,
as mostly I've forgotten how to weep ... Only mostly, though,

sometimes I can sense the tears in there, and sometimes, yes,
they flow, though rarely for a reason I'd have thought –
a cello's voice will catch in mine, a swerve in a poem, and once,
a death, someone I hardly knew, but I found myself sobbing, sobbing,
for everyone I had known who'd died, and some who almost had.

In the next display hall, evolution: half, the quarter creatures,
Australopithecus, Pithecanthropus, Cro-Magnon,
sidle diffidently along their rocky winding path towards us.
Flint and fire, science and song, and all of it coming to this,
this unhealable self in myself who knows what I should know.

RICHARD PRICE

Wake Up and Sleep

The thought keeps counting

The weight of my own eyes.
I have a forehead. A mouth,
dry. The thought –

the thought the thought the thought

*

Overheated. A wash of the face
and it's right cold if you run the tap.

*

A drink of the old polar covalent,
ache too oh. Simple. Can work.

*

Not this time.

*

the thought the thought the thought

*

Drowsy in charge of a photocopier.

'Off coffee, thanks.'

The tea's buzzless, camomile and calm.
I'm gulping watercolours, columnists' remedies.

*

the thought

*

The thought keeps counting. Can the thought
just stop counting?

*

Lives in the linear programming, people in the detail.

*

the thought the thought

*

Drowsy in charge of a people carrier.

*

The night's A–Z is stuck at Why.
Anyone know Zed Street?

'In your dreams.'

*

With primary insomnia the data suggests
there's *decreased* regional cerebral blood flow (rCBF)
to the frontal medial, occipital, and parietal cortices,
and to the basal ganglia. I'll explain these things later.
Countries of the brain. Decrease, yes. Surprising
when you don't think about it.

We know behaviour therapy for insomnia (BT-I) works
but how does it work? Definitive conclusions
are just not possible but first indications –
it's just one study – but first indications
suggest successful treatment is associated

(I have to emphasise it's an association at this point),
with a *reversal* in cerebral deactivation.

*

the thought the thought the thought

*

The thought was only thinking,
the thought just doesn't think.

You just don't think, do you?

*

They were diagnosed through interviews,
psychometrics, blood chemistries, sleep diaries.

Subjects underwent three nights of polysomnographic testing
and on Night 3, ten minutes after the first K-complex / sleep
        spindle
they were infused with 25mCi of Tc-99m-HMPAO.

Sorry, yes, infused means injected.

Twelve minutes after injection we woke the subjects up.
They were scanned.

Subjects then completed an eight-session per week BT-I protocol
which included sleep restriction and stimulus control.
We repeated the three-night imaging procedure
(single photon emission computed tomography,
SPECT).

On diary measures, all patients exhibited improvements in sleep
(including, in layman's terms, falling to sleep quicker, night
        wakenings fewer).

The SPECT results you know:
while it appears that insomnia may be experienced by the sufferer
as thinking too much – the behaviour of 'a worrier'
or, temporarily, a victim of inspiration –
objective analysis associates this variety of sleeplessness
with reduced cerebral activity.

A healthy sleeper has a lively sleeping mind?

*

Behavioural therapy does tend to work,
but unlearning the anxiety of the bedroom is perhaps seen as 'not
        medical'.
It is certainly expensive. Funding sessions with a sleep therapist
would give the Health Service sleepless nights.

Zed drugs are cheap to make, cheap to administer.
They are effective, for as long as they are taken. Then: to break the
        pattern.
In sleep medicine, Zed is the last word.

*

The last word.

Sleep, be your kindness.
Kindle slumber now. Let tenderness and balm be your touching
        flames.
Consume unthinking thought. Welcome me this anxious night
with gentle oblivion.

*

Drowsy in charge of

Drowsy in charge of

Drowsy in charge of
a king-sized kingdom of good nights.

'Night.'

Continuous Positive Air Pressure

My age your muscles are under more strain. They're in the neck, like guy ropes. Yes I like a sandwich, a lemon shandy. Snoresville, but I didn't know it. 'Please wake up and pipe down.' My clothes are tentish, too, 'My buffalo pavilion.'

Obstructive apnoea: long-suffering partners hawsering their long-haul snufflers in. The livids and the oblivious.

The endurance of affection is a marriage, all kinds of sleeplessness and it is a killer. A classic motorway accident – waking in the swerve – or a door banging across the hours, not quite each, not quite every minute.

Tonight I settle with a mask on my face, captain of the jet, and the compressor gives you breath, a mask on my face waiting (we're both loaded with waiting, 'Remember, the bedroom is not a fearful place'). We're waiting for the flight, for the benevolent stratosphere of nothing. We're waiting to cross goodnight's tender continent of out-for-the-count. In this luxury liner from first officer to passenger we measure the currency in dreams. We are millionaires.

Wake up and sleep

Drowsy finalising the blueprint,
drowsy verifying the footprint.
Drowsy in data entry,
drowsy on checkpoint sentry,
drowsy and missing the asset-stripping on Dead Street.

Half-asleep, fingertipping the spreadsheet,
thumbing the defective directory
of on-the-mind on-the-mend half-attended ex's.
Half-asleep and just holding on
to the handholds in the homemade purgatory
of six-of-one custody fro-and-to vexes.
Half asleep quoting chapter and hexes
from the ratified sleepwalking directive.

Wake up outside your conscientious waking dream,
wake up and sleep.
Wake up outside your ache, your late luscious just-what-it-seems,
wake up and sleep.
Wake up to the what-happened, wake up to the casehardened,
wake up between look and leap.
Wake up in the shatter and decade-seep,
wake up and sleep.

Say goodnight to shaking –
there's a wake in over-waking.
Scowls and scarlatina are the stories in the clinic cantina:
more at the morgue does tend to mean less.
Owls and the ocarina are glories in the night's arena
but leave them for a week, I guess.
(Sleep's demeanour improves life's fever –
you need to nod to get to yes.)

Peace and quiet for the codes and the kids,
for the didn't-halfs and the nearly-dids. Rest your roads, your
    well-rids.
Peace and quiet for the sky-deep, ocean-high equation.
No tended-baggage advantage-adage panic profiticians. No
    palpitations.
Peace and quiet for the offence-taking nations-within-nations.
Peace. Not a peep. Please,
sleep.

SYLVIA PLATH

Fever 103°

Pure? What does it mean?
The tongues of hell
Are dull, dull as the triple

Tongues of dull, fat Cerberus
Who wheezes at the gate. Incapable
Of licking clean

The aguey tendon, the sin, the sin.
The tinder cries.
The indelible smell

Of a snuffed candle!
Love, love, the low smokes roll
From me like Isadora's scarves, I'm in a fright

One scarf will catch and anchor in the wheel.
Such yellow sullen smokes
Make their own element. They will not rise,

But trundle round the globe
Choking the aged and the meek,
The weak

Hothouse baby in its crib,
The ghastly orchid
Hanging its hanging garden in the air,

Devilish leopard!
Radiation turned it white
And killed it in an hour.

Greasing the bodies of adulterers
Like Hiroshima ash and eating in.
The sin. The sin.

Darling, all night
I have been flickering, off, on, off, on.
The sheets grow heavy as a lecher's kiss.

Three days. Three nights.
Lemon water, chicken
Water, water make me retch.

I am too pure for you or anyone.
Your body
Hurts me as the world hurts God. I am a lantern –

My head a moon
Of Japanese paper, my gold beaten skin
Infinitely delicate and infinitely expensive.

Does not my heat astound you. And my light.
All by myself I am a huge camellia
Glowing and coming and going, flush on flush.

I think I am going up,
I think I may rise –
The beads of hot metal fly, and I, love, I

Am a pure acetylene .
Virgin
Attended by roses,

By kisses, by cherubim,
By whatever these pink things mean.
Not you, nor him

Not him, nor him
(My selves dissolving, old whore petticoats) –
To Paradise.

JACQUES RÉDA

The Soul's Situation

The flesh, yes, but the soul has no desire for eternity,
Shrinking like a rounded breath
On the pane, a mere syncope
In the lengthy phrase the gods breathe out.
It knows it is mortal and almost imaginary
And rejoices as such in secret away from the torturing heart.
It's how a child who is kept from playing
Slips away, eyes lowered against his own transparency.
But where are the gods, poor things? – In the cellar;
And they only come up at night, to look in the garbage
For a bit to eat. The gods
Have turned the corner on the street. The gods
Humbly order a toddy at the station bar
And throw up at daybreak against a tree. The gods
Would willingly die. (But only the soul can,
At a distance from the gods and the fretful body
In its eternity of nitrogen and hydrogen,
At a distance dance an airy death.)

translated by Jennie Feldman

CHRISTOPHER REID

from The Unfinished

11
So like a baby,
with her bald head
and one working arm
clear of the blanket
that the ambulance men
had folded her in,
but a baby with wide, wise,
learning eyes
and an unexpected
gift of speech,
she proceeded first
to puzzle, then charm,
her attendants with a burst
of questions and comments
on everything in reach:
from the gadgets and fixtures
to the colour of her blanket,
a pragmatic scarlet;
then, as the vehicle
speeded along,
the swivelling, wrong-
way-round, receding
view through the window
of sky and the tops
of trees and shops,
which made a familiar
route hard to follow;
via this, that and the other,
till – how, I can't think –

they were onto the subject
of favourite drinks,
and no one objected
when she nominated
as the most delicious
of all, champagne.

TOM PAULIN

A Lyric Afterwards

There was a taut dryness all that summer
and you sat each day in the hot garden
until those uniformed comedians
filled the street with their big white ambulance,
fetching you and bringing you back to me.

Far from the sea of ourselves we waited
and prayed for the tight blue silence to give.
In your absence I climbed to a square room
where there were dried flowers, folders of sonnets
and crossword puzzles: call them musical

snuffboxes or mannered anachronisms,
they were all too uselessly intricate,
caskets of the dead spirit. Their bitter
constraints and formal pleasures were a style
of being perfect in despair; they spoke

with the vicious trapped crying of a wren.
But that is changed now, and when I see you
walking by the river, a step from me,
there is this great kindness everywhere:
now in the grace of the world and always.

Notes on Denise Riley's 'Pancreas, Liver, Biliary Tract', page 73

i Urology was an elaborate art, and a diagnostic tool when other resources were few. Shakespeare writes of the practice in *King Henry the Fourth*, Part II:

FALSTAFF: Sirrah, you giant, what says the doctor to my water?

PAGE: He said, sir, the water was a good healthy water; but for the party that owned it, he might have more diseases than he bargained for.

ii The subtitle of Robert Burton's *Anatomy of Melancholy*, 1621: 'What it is, With all the kinds, causes, symptoms, prognostics, and several cures of it, Philosophically, Medicinally, Historically opened and cut up.'

iii Pancreatitis begins when the digestive enzymes become active inside the pancreas itself and start 'digesting' it.

iv In acute pancreatitis, the blood contains at least three times more amylase and lipase than usual. (These are the digestive enzymes formed in the pancreas.)

v For Galen, *c.* AD 200, the liver was the seat of the vegetal spirit: 'Now, why is the stomach surrounded by the liver? Is it in order that the liver may warm it and it may in turn warm the food? This is indeed the very reason why it is closely clasped by the lobes of the liver, as if by fingers.' Medieval manuscripts show digestive processes as internal cooking. The stomach sat above the liver like a pot over a fire. The liver was chief cook, but if it undercooked the food or burned it, dire consequences ensued.

vi From Pablo Neruda's *Ode to the Liver*.

vii In 1653 William Harvey termed the liver as a 'noble organ' and the spleen an 'ignoble organ'. The gall bladder was 'a very long pear compressed from base into neck' and the spleen 'like the tongue of an ox [or] the sole of the foot; slightly bowed out on the left side, a little concave on the inner side, toward the stomach. It has an uneven surface and is a little rough with some tubercles.'

viii 'The sanguine man hath good appetite, and quick digestion; his urine is yellow and thick, his pulse is great and full, and dreameth of red things, and pleasant conceits.' From *Astrological Judgement of Diseases from the Decumbiture of the Sick*, Nicholas Culpeper, 1655.

ix   Bile, or gall, is a bitter fluid secreted by the liver, stored in the gallbladder. Diseases sprang from disturbances of the balance of the humours, the body fluids: blood, phlegm, yellow bile and black bile. Galen held that the gall bladder, spleen and liver produced and stored three of the four humours of the body: blood (liver), yellow bile (gallbladder) and black bile (spleen). The very word melancholy means 'black bile'.

x   Lamentations, book 3, verse 19, The Bible, King James version.

xi   Gall, or bile, emulsifies fats in the intestines. Wormwood was regarded as a remedy for liver, gallbladder, stomach and liver disorders, and for worm infestations. Its constituents include the bitter absinthin, a narcotic analgesic used in vermouth, and absinthe, which became popular in the late 1880s to early 1900s. Absinthe manufacture was established by Henri-Louis Pernod in 1797.

xii Two modern signs of rampaging enzymes, in severe acute pancreatitis. The Cullen sign is a bluish skin discoloration around the navel, the Grey-Turner sign a reddish-brown discoloration.

xiii I am grateful for this information to Professor Roger Williams.

Notes on the Commissioned Poems

Moniza Alvi on 'Post-Traumatic', page 94

I've had a long-standing interest in Post-Traumatic Stress Disorder, knew something of its Pandora's Box of symptoms, and also how it could strike many years after a traumatic happening. I'd read some helpful books, for example Caroline Garland's *Understanding Trauma* (Karnac 2002), and was fascinated to have the opportunity to talk with David Sturgeon at University College Hospital about his experiences of trying to 'contain' the illness. I asked about memory and repression, and what might happen physiologically, and he very helpfully suggested a conversation between the mind and the brain. I also wondered about how recovery might be identified, and David mentioned 'a love of life'. I found this moving.

Maura Dooley on 'STENT!', page 112

Thomas Hardy's poem 'Heredity' begins,

> *I am the family face;*
> *Flesh perishes, I live on,*
> *Projecting trait and trace*
> *Through time to times anon,*
> *And leaping from place to place,*
> *Over oblivion.*

I have watched my young daughter develop mannerisms and behaviour patterns very like those of her Grandfather, dead many years before she was born. There are other combinations of genes in my family that have thrown up several unusual medical conditions, more serious and more troubling. I set out to understand something more about genetics. However, research, like the writing of poetry, takes unexpected turns. In the course of thinking and reading about one condition, my husband unexpectedly developed another and suddenly, of necessity, I found myself reading studies of the heart. The poem I ended up with pushed its way through because the process of angioplasty presented such an obvious and immediate comparison to the process of editing.

Ian Duhig on 'love me little', page 90

'Learn to glory in a Stranger' – Wordsworth, 'The White Doe of Rylstone'. I have written previously about autism, but felt even closer to this commission when during research I read (in Baron-Cohen and Bolton among others) that its sufferers often display great interest in etymology as well as poetry – I already knew they may grasp information more easily given in verse rather than as prose. Elsewhere, I frequently encountered such phrases as 'weak central coherence' to describe their unusual systemisations of knowledge; however, my adviser warned me of how provisional medical understanding in this area is at present, so I also read autobiographies of people with autism and talked to caseworkers for alternative dimensions. All this plus the Deleuzoguattarian rhizome model (co-opted against arborescent central coherence) went into my poem, which I hoped would demonstrate eccentric but not irrational organising principles (/s for rhymes etc.), that with a little lateral thinking would reveal an individual voice, as with meeting a stranger for the first time.

Grey Gowrie on 'Local', page 89

'Local' is one of a sequence of poems about a year spent in hospital when I was awaiting or recovering from a heart transplant. E Ward is Harefield's home for the most seriously afflicted.

David Harsent on 'Tinnitus', page 51

I woke up, one morning some six or seven years ago, with bipolar tinnitus. During the course of the day, I waited for it to go away: it didn't; and it hasn't. Sometimes a fluctuating whine in my head, sometimes a scream, sometimes shrill, sometimes more distant, sometimes something underlying all of that: footsteps on gravel, the sound of the sea. I carry it everywhere all the time. A demon on my shoulder. A machine strapped to my back. It waits for me while I sleep. It's toughing me out.

W.N. Herbert on 'Revenant', page 108

Fifteen years ago I lived in a terraced house in East Oxford that had previously belonged to a photographer. He had lived there for many years with his mother, developing a drink problem so severe that after her death he was sectioned. The house had been painted a wild range of colours, there was evidence of blood on the walls, a warren of old brick outhouses out the back, and a distinctly unpleasant presence. We cleaned, repainted, demolished, exorcised, and were very happy. Then there came a knocking at the door. Somehow the photographer had left his asylum, and walked home in his slippers. Speechless, but still equipped with a map both of the route to his home and of its former interior, he went and lay down in our kitchen, his old workroom. The nurses came, apologised, and fetched him back. This happened several times, and each time they reiterated that he was harmless, and that he had very little sense of who we were or indeed who he was. And the more they explained this, the more I came to see his homing instinct as the most extraordinary survival mechanism. When there was apparently nothing else left, he could still find his way home. I wondered if I would be able to do the same.

Kathleen Jamie on 'The Pathologist', page 43

I asked to do Pathology because of my previous experience visiting, and writing about, the Pathology Museum at the Royal College of Surgeons in Edinburgh. Having spent plenty of time among the ancient dead body-parts preserved in jars, I thought it would be appropriate to discover what modern pathologists do. Professor Carey kindly showed me round the labs at Ninewells, in Dundee. In my ignorance I'd been expecting corpses, but of course there were none. There were samples, even whole organs, being minutely examined. I learned that Pathology is a service by and for the living, to keep us that way.

Jackie Kay on 'My Face is a Map', page 37

I've always been interested in facial deformity because our society is so obsessed with how people look. I've wondered how difficult it is to get past the prejudices to communicate with people, and be seen for yourself and not your so-called deformity. Working with Iain Hutchison of Saving Faces was incredibly rewarding and interesting, but I then almost ended up with too much information to find a way into my poem. Only when I seemed to let go of the facts, could the poem come, and then so much of what I'd learnt fed back into the poem. I'd learnt that children who feel very loved and whose parents have always made them feel special have a better chance at coping with their faces than children whose parents are constantly trying to get them plastic surgery. I also learnt a bit about the dilemma of whether or not to accept plastic surgery, whether or not to reconstruct the self. When I came up with the idea of the face as a map of Australia, I was away. Before that I'd written several unsuccessful poems that were weighed down with the research. I wanted to write the poem in the voice of a child, I imagined a twelve-year-old child, because it felt fresher and more immediate, and because of that I think of 'My Face is a Map' as a children's poem.

Stephen Knight on 'The Nightingale Standard', page 136

'The Nightingale Standard' was constructed from material found in *The Family Physician* (The Caxton Publishing Company, second edition, 1951), revised by M. MacKenzie M.B., Ch.B., with contributions by Specialists and edited by a leading Medical Authority.

Michael Laskey on 'Early Morning Waking', page 134

Looking at this poem again, I realise now how closely it's related to Larkin's 'The Building'. Behind my poem stands his hospital 'higher than the handsomest hotel', and the boy I focus on may well be a direct descendent of his patient 'wheeled past, in washed-to-rags ward clothes'. But whereas Larkin's slowly unfolding tour of the hospital steels us to face 'the coming dark', mine is more of a prayer, written in the hope that my concentration on the words, the tight stanzas, may somehow help the boy. As if my waking up early to write – by far the best time, I find – might in some sense counter-balance or alleviate his early morning waking.

Gwyneth Lewis on 'Glaucoma', page 154

I chose Ophthalmology as the medical specialism I'd like to know more about because my mother is slowly losing her sight to glaucoma and because I'm slightly colour blind myself. I've always been both fascinated and repulsed by the eye, as it's so soft and vulnerable. When I met ophthalmologist Dr James Morgan at Cardiff University, he pointed out that the eye is the one organ that we can't see. At the time of writing this poem, I was Poet in Residence in the Department of Physics and Astronomy at Cardiff, so I was fascinated when Professor Fred Fitzke of University College London, who had studied cosmology himself, told me that, if you colour the cells in the eye, watching them light up as they commit suicide is exactly like watching stars. So, I imagined supernovae dimming in my mother's eyes, as she struggles, these days, to knit with dark wool.

Carola Luther on 'I watch the bees slow down the summer', page 82

I found looking into the subject of getting very old more depressing than I expected. But despite the scientific details of what happens to the body and brain as we age, despite newspaper stories of under-funded nursing homes and unsatisfactory services for older people, despite what many believe to be a culture of disrespect for the elderly, despite reports of loneliness and poverty and ill health, something stubbornly 'otherwise' remained. Not least this was due to the elderly people I have known and loved, and many others whose creativity, subversiveness, wit, and resourcefulness I have heard or read about. After learning some particularly daunting facts about dementia, and the treatment for strokes, I asked John Young of St Luke's Hospital, Bradford, why he so valued working with the elderly. He thought for a moment and said: 'I can honestly say that if I'm ever in a bad a mood when I get to work, spending time with my elderly patients will lift that mood.' It seemed to me that John was describing a kind of gift, something subtle and gentle and unexpected that the very old give us. It was partly from this thought that my poem came.

Jamie McKendrick on 'Darkness Tangible', page 58

Perhaps foolishly, I didn't take advantage of the kind offer to speak with a consultant. With my father having been a cardiologist and my mother a doctor, I'd constantly overheard the Latin and Greek of medical discourse – from myocardial infarctions to beta blockers – and am still partial to its music. But for the purposes of this poem I wanted to take another direction – more physical than medical, perhaps more dream-like than actual.

Daljit Nagra on 'Booking Khan Singh Kumar', page 126

This poem arises from the schizophrenic situation where the character feels he is thinking and writing in a language that he doesn't feel is his, and is using the traditions of a culture that he feels are not necessarily his. This accommodated fracture of the self is exemplified by even his name which is a chaos of common Muslim, Sikh and Hindu names that share a violent history. In the foreign tradition, the character feels he is a representation who is devoid of specificity and considers whether he is the exploited or the exploiter.

Sean O'Brien on 'The Hand', page 101

Dupuytren's Contracture is recurrent and incurable and involves a build-up of debris in the sheaths of tendons in the hand. The effect is gradually to claw the affected finger(s) into the palm. Margaret Thatcher suffers from this complaint. I trust this is all we have in common.

I had operations on my right hand in 1997, my left in 1999, and my right again in 2004. Since the last procedure my right hand has suffered reduced flexibility and grip. Fortunately I'm left-handed.

In writing the poem I was intrigued by the idea of having to make what was in effect a strategic withdrawal from part of the body, as well as by the obvious overtones of mortality, and by the relationship of body and mind. So it's been a rich experience, although I wish I could still deal easily with small coins on the bus.

Ruth Padel on 'The Origins of Malaria', page 65

I wanted to explore what the malaria parasite does in the system of both the mosquito and the human being, how it affects people socially, physically, economically. The city and the forest; everything. Malaria is caused by protozoan parasites, of the genus *Plasmodium*, transmitted from one person to another by the female anopheline mosquito. The parasite is developing immunity to all the chemicals currently used to control it by attacking it at some stage of its cycle. I went to talk to two inspirational researchers. Dr Crisanti, an immunologist at Imperial College London, is doing cutting edge research based, as far as I understood it, on the idea of modifying the mosquito genetically (they breed so fast, that if you released some of these modified ones they would take over eventually). So far he's managed to make their testicles glow. Which apparently shows it could be done. But what he wants to do is modify their cells so they are aware that a parasite has entered their body, and eject it. Then I went to Dr Jean Langhorne, who works in the Division of Parasitology in the National Institute for Medical Research. Jean showed me on her screen exactly how *Plasmodium* works, the whole cycle of the malarial parasite in detail, how it explodes in the red cells in the most disgusting and dramatic and successful way. For this poem, the key thing you have to know is that the malaria parasite sneakily develops in the mosquito gut and then gets out and breaks down the cells in the liver and blood of the next host. It does seem a sort of sci fi parable of evil: like Satan in *Paradise Lost* deciding to get back at God by attacking this new creature He has created, Man.

Richard Price on 'Wake Up and Sleep', page 171

The first section of 'Wake Up and Sleep' deals with the sleeplessness that many will have experienced: the sense of not being able to 'switch off', a feeling that can become quite desperate if repeated once or twice in a short space of days. The sufferer may not think of worry as the trigger and might experience it instead as a kind of thought-repetition that will not allow slumber, a stopping of thought's processes by thought itself. Soon sleeplessness itself becomes a worry, however, and so the potential for a downward spiral. I've adapted research texts and tried to evoke drug treatments and cognitive therapies. I am not a realist and I have adapted freely but not, I hope, grievously. The second section features obstructive apnoea. I did not know anything about this very common sleep disorder and here a prose poem emerged as a way of folding in different ideas and effects that were suggested to me by my reading on the topic, by my conversation with Dr Peter Venn at the Queen Victoria Hospital in East Grinstead, and by the section itself as I wrote and re-wrote it. The last section of the poem departs from the strictly medical brief. It is written in a sprung, strongly rhymed and assonated form which seemed more suited to a widening and concluding public address and to the feverishness of a nation it characterises as unable to sleep.

Denise Riley on 'Pancreas, Liver, Biliary Tract', page 73

I'd originally thought I'd write about speech disturbances and aphasiology, matters in which I'd long been interested. But then an unexpected spell in hospital intervened, most helpfully, to furnish me with this new subject. Professor Roger Williams, Director of the Institute of Hepatology, University College London, kindly agreed to talk to me about the work of the Institute, and the current state of research on liver and biliary tract conditions.

Robin Robertson on 'A Seagull Murmur', page 54

Murmurs are abnormal heart sounds that are produced as a result of blood turbulence through a valve, which is sufficient to produce audible noise. This most commonly results from narrowing or leaking of valves or the presence of abnormal passages through which blood flows in or near the heart. In certain patients, the murmur sometimes has a high-pitched musical or raucous quality – termed 'a seagull murmur'.

Replacement of the aortic valve requires open-heart surgery, in which the sternum is split down the middle, allowing access to the heart. The heart is stopped during critical parts of the operation and a bypass machine supports the body by pumping it through with oxygenated blood. The incompetent valve is removed and a prosthetic one sewn in. The mechanical valve makes a clicking noise when closing that may be heard when the room is quiet or when listening near the chest.

Ann Sansom on 'On Psoriasis', page 149

I was pleased to be asked to write for this project, though admittedly there were a number of times I regretted picking the psoriasis, as it were. A bit close to home. And frankly, it wasn't my first choice. I ticked it only because it was familiar territory. The trouble I had was trying to write while pulling together things I didn't want to acknowledge but had nevertheless explored and, for the purposes of this, reinforced in a brief chat with Jonathan Barker at St John's Institute of Dermatology. Yes. I know. The parallel with writing seems obvious, to writers at least. Relentless temptation, capitulation, making a mess of the sheets, covering up, getting found out. For John Updike it was a mansion of hidden delights. I can see his point. Psoriasis is the body's way of saying *farewell to flesh*, carnivale. But speaking too enthusiastically, too desperately. Seems a bit harsh to be excommunicated *and* burned alive for that. It's alright now. Cortisones. And the Armadillo's had a word with the Church on our behalf.

Jo Shapcott on 'Composition', page 98

The poem 'Composition' was written as a result of meetings with Neurophysiologist Dr Mark Lythgoe, Director of the Biomedical Imaging Centre at University College London and Senior Lecturer at the UCL Institute of Child Health. One of the most fascinating ideas he introduced me to is the concept of latent inhibition, which came up during a conversation about creativity – a special interest of his. Mark has described latent inhibition as 'the ability we all have to filter out irrelevant stimuli. Thus we can read a book, walk down the street and hold a conversation, or go to sleep in a noisy room. Yet this ability may hold back our creativity. It appears that creative people are prone to be flooded with irrelevant thoughts and ideas [and] lowering your filtering threshold to allow the mind to wander may permit information to pour in in an oblique way, facilitating the making of extraordinary associations.' (From Mark Lythgoe, 'Reawakening the Creative Mind', *The New Statesman*, 3rd October, 2005.) As an account of what it feels like to write a poem, Mark's description seemed to me spot on. 'Composition' emerged as an attempt to give an account of the many 'irrelevant thoughts' and external impressions occurring during the making of a poem. I tried to make the poem a 'real time' experience for the reader so that it appears (I hope!) to be a record of what went on in the mind of the poet as it happened, culminating in the final, surprising 'this' which is, of course, the poem itself.

Greta Stoddart on 'Want', page 145

The subject of infertility wasn't my first choice. I had mixed feelings about it as I'd been trying for a (second) child for two years and had thought myself into a corner. But the first four lines came quickly, and very clearly, in the voice of an unconceived child. By the time I'd finished the poem I was pregnant – after, incidentally, following the rather reckless advice offered by the child in the poem.

Acknowledgements

I would like to thank the Calouste Gulbenkian Foundation, and in particular Siân Ede, for devising, facilitating and funding this project, and Felicity Luard and Louisa Hooper for overseeing the publication of this book. I am also grateful to the Royal Society of Medicine for their assistance and support.

Particular thanks are also due to Siân Ede, Jo Parkinson at the Royal Society of Medicine, Roseanna Hargreaves, Guy's Hospital, London, and Charlotte Feinmann, University College Hospital, London, for their assistance in finding medical experts to work with poets.

The following is a list of the poets and their medical collaborators to whom we are grateful for their generosity with their time, expertise and advice.

Moniza Alvi: David Sturgeon, Consultant Liaison Psychiatrist, University College Hospital, London

Ian Duhig: Tony Charman, Reader in Neurodevelopmental Disorders, Behavioural and Brain Sciences Unit, Institute of Child Health, University College London

W.N. Herbert: Julian Hughes, Consultant in Old Age Psychiatry, North Tyneside General Hospital

Kathleen Jamie: Frank Carey, Clinical Leader in Pathology, NHS Tayside, Ninewells Hospital, Dundee

Jackie Kay: Iain Hutchison, Consultant Oral and Maxillofacial Surgeon, St Bartholomew's Hospital, London

Michael Laskey: Jeffrey Brain, Consultant Paediatric Surgeon, Addenbrookes Hospital, Cambridge University Hospitals

Gwyneth Lewis: Fred Fitzke, Professor of Visual Optics and Psychophysics, Department of Visual Science, Institute of Ophthalmology, University College London, Wendy Franks, Director of the Glaucoma Service at the Moorfields Eye Hospital, London, and James Morgan, Reader in Ophthalmology, Cardiff University, and Honorary Consultant Ophthalmologist, University Hospital of Wales.

Carola Luther: John Young, Department of Elderly Care, St Luke's Hospital, Bradford, and Rosie Larner, a carer for many years of an elderly person with Alzheimer's.

Daljit Nagra: Sheilagh Davies, Consultant Psychiatrist in Psychotherapy, Maudsley Hospital, London

Ruth Padel: Jean Langhorne, Division of Parasitology, National Institute for Medical Research, London, and Andrea Crisanti, Department of Biological Sciences, Imperial College London

Richard Price: Peter Venn, Directory of the Sleep Studies Unit, Queen Victoria Hospital, East Grinstead

Denise Riley: Roger Williams, Director of the Institute of Hepatology, University College London

Ann Sansom: Jonathan Barker, St John's Institute of Dermatology, King's College Hospital, London

Jo Shapcott: Mark Lythgoe, Director of the Biomedical Imaging Centre, University College London, and Senior Lecturer at the UCL Institute of Child Health

Greta Stoddart: Ruth Curson, Fertility Consultant, King's College Hospital, London

The other commissioned poets were: Maura Dooley, Grey Gowrie, David Harsent, Stephen Knight, Jamie McKendrick, Sean O'Brien, Robin Robertson.

The editor and the Calouste Gulbenkian Foundation would like to thank the following poets and publishers for permission to reproduce their work:

Simon Armitage, 'Book of Matches: Ankylosing spondilitis' from *Selected Poems* (Faber and Faber Ltd 2001) and 'Splinter' from *The Universal Home Doctor* (Faber and Faber Ltd 2002); John Berryman, 'Dream Song 207: How Are You?' from *The Dream Songs* (Faber and Faber Ltd 1990); John Betjeman, 'Devonshire Street W1' from *Collected Poems*, copyright © The Estate of John Betjeman, reproduced by permission of John Murray (Publishers) Ltd; Raymond Carver, 'What the Doctor Said' from *All of Us: Collected Poems*, published by Harvill Press, © Tess Gallagher, reprinted by permission of The Random House Group Ltd; Polly Clarke, 'Cheng du Massage' from *Take Me With You* (Bloodaxe Books 2005); Lucille Clifton, 'to my last period' from *Blessing the Boats: New and Selected Poems 1988–2000*, © 1991, 2000 by Lucille

Clifton, reprinted with the permission of BOA Editions, Ltd; Fred D'Aguiar, 'Airy Hall Ward' from *Airy Hall* and 'Obeah Mama Dot' from *Mama Dot*, published by Chatto and Windus, reprinted by permission of The Random House Group Ltd; Julia Darling, 'Chemotherapy' from *Sudden Collapses in Public Places* (Arc 2003); Ian Duhig, 'From the Plague Journal', reprinted by permission of the poet; Douglas Dunn, 'Thirteen Steps and the Thirteenth of March' from *New Selected Poems 1964–2000* (Faber and Faber Ltd 2003); Leontia Flynn, 'Acts of Faith' from *These Days*, published by Jonathan Cape, reprinted by permission of The Random House Group Ltd; Cheryl Follon, 'Madam Aphrodisia' from *All Your Talk* (Bloodaxe Books 2004); Thom Gunn, 'Memory Unsettled' from *The Man with the Night Sweats* (Faber and Faber Ltd 1992); Ian Hamilton, 'Admission', 'Awakening' and 'The Visit' from *Fifty Poems* (Faber and Faber Ltd 1988), reprinted by permission of Gillon Aitken Associates; Robert Hass, 'A Story About the Body' from *Human Wishes*, © 1989 by Robert Hass, reprinted by permission of HarperCollins Publishers; Zbigniew Herbert, 'The Hygiene of the Soul' (7 lines) from *Selected Poems*, p. 120, translated by Czeslaw Milosz and Peter Dale Scott (Penguin Books, London 1968), translation copyright © Czeslaw Milosz and Peter Dale Scott, 1968, reproduced by permission of Penguin Books Ltd; Bob Hicok, 'Alzheimer's' from *Plus Shipping*, © 1998 by Bob Hicok, reprinted with the permission of BOA Editions, Ltd; Selima Hill, 'Nothing' from *Bunny* (Bloodaxe Books 2001) and an extract from 'The Inpatient, Chapter 3: Doctors' from *Trembling Hearts in the Bodies of Dogs* (Bloodaxe Books 1994); Miroslav Holub, 'Brief reflection on the word Pain' from *Poems Before & After* (Bloodaxe Books 2006); Horace, 'Epodes 3: Parentis olim' (37 lines) from *The Complete Odes and Epodes with the Centennial Hymn*, p. 50, translated with notes by W.G. Shepherd, introduction by Betty Radice (Penguin Classics, London 1983), translation copyright © W.G. Shepherd, 1983, introduction copyright © Betty Radice, 1983, reproduced by permission of Penguin Books Ltd; Alan Jenkins, 'Launderette: Her Last Nightdress' from *A Shorter Life*, published by Chatto and Windus, reprinted by permission of The Random House Group Ltd; Jackie Kay, 'Dance of the Cherry Blossom' from *The Adoption Papers* (Bloodaxe Books 2003); Philip Larkin, 'Ambulances' from *Collected Poems* (Faber and Faber Ltd 1988); James Lasdun, 'Plague Years' from *The Revenant*, published by Jonathan Cape, reprinted by permission of The Random House

Index of Poets

Lavinia Greenlaw

Lavinia Greenlaw is a poet and novelist who comes from a family of doctors and scientists. She has published three books of poems, most recently *Minsk* (Faber 2003), which was shortlisted for the Forward, T.S. Eliot and Whitbread Poetry Prizes, and two novels, *Mary George of Allnorthover* (Flamingo 2001), which won France's Prix du Premier Roman, and *An Irresponsible Age* (Fourth Estate 2006). She has also collaborated with the photographic artist Garry Fabian Miller on *Thoughts of a Night Sea* (Merrell 2003) and written her first book of non-fiction, *The Importance of Music to Girls* (Faber 2007). Other awards include a Forward Prize, a Cholmondeley Award, an Arts Council England Writer's Award, and a fellowship from the National Endowment for Science, Technology and the Arts (NESTA). Lavinia Greenlaw teaches at Goldsmiths College, University of London and is a Fellow of the Royal Society of Literature.

Also published by the Calouste Gulbenkian Foundation

Wild Reckoning: An anthology provoked by Rachel Carson's Silent Spring
Edited by John Burnside and Maurice Riordan

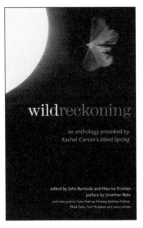

Wild Reckoning is an anthology inspired by the fortieth anniversary of Rachel Carson's controversial and prophetic book *Silent Spring*, which warned against the indiscriminate use of pesticides and consequences for the environment. The anthology features poems commissioned from leading poets – including Simon Armitage, Paul Farley, Linda Gregerson and Deryn Rees-Jones – which were the fruit of discussions with scientists such as Richard Fortey and John Sulston. It also brings to the fore poems, both contemporary and from the past, which, while belonging in the great tradition of English nature poetry, express a concern for the fragility of living things.

A Poetry Book Society Special Commendation, *Wild Reckoning* was chosen by the Government's Chief Scientific Adviser, Sir David King, to take to his imaginary Desert Island.

£7.50 pbk ISBN 978 1 903080 00 9 (2004)

Available from Central Books, 99 Wallis Road, London E9 5LN
Tel: 0845 458 9911, Fax: 0845 458 9912
Website: www.centralbooks.co.uk